# outdoor food

OVER 80 MOUTHWATERING RECIPES
FOR PARTIES AND BARBECUES

LINDA DOESER

This is a Parragon Publishing Book
First published in 2004

Parragon Publishing
Queen Street House
4 Queen Street
Bath BA1 1HE, UK

Created and produced for Parragon by The Bridgewater Book Company Ltd.

ISBN: 1-40543-268-3

Printed in China

*NOTE*
*This book uses imperial, metric, and US cup measurements. Follow the same units of
measurement throughout; do not mix imperial and metric. All spoon measurements
are level: teaspoons are assumed to be 5 ml and tablespoons are assumed to be 15 ml.
Unless otherwise stated, milk is assumed to be whole, eggs and individual vegetables
such as potatoes are medium, and pepper is freshly ground black pepper.*

*The times given for each recipe are an approximate guide only. Cooking times
may vary as a result of the type of oven used. Ovens should be preheated to the
specified temperature. If using a fan-assisted oven, check the manufacturer's
instructions for adjusting the time and temperature.*

*Recipes using raw or very lightly cooked eggs should be avoided by infants, the elderly,
pregnant women, convalescents, and anyone suffering from an illness. Pregnant and
breastfeeding women are advised to avoid eating peanuts and peanut products.*

# Contents

# Introduction

Sharing food with family and friends has always been one of the greatest pleasures of life and, when combined with all the fun of eating in the open air, it becomes twice as enjoyable. There are lots of ways to enjoy alfresco food without wearing yourself out in advance, such as a simple gathering of friends in the backyard on a summer evening, an afternoon picnic by the lake, or an informal portable barbecue

brunch on the beach. More substantial parties are great, too, and don't have to be a hard slog, whether an elegant evening buffet or a full-scale, three-course barbecue for 20.

Careful planning is the secret of success and this book is packed with fabulous recipes and clever ideas for just such occasions. Whether you intend to

serve cold food or hot snacks or to cook on the grill, most of the work will be completed before your guests arrive, giving you time to catch up with each other's news—and to check that everyone is supplied with a drink.

This book is divided into two main sections. The first offers practical, general advice on entertaining, plus three chapters of great recipes for hot and cold

snacks, dips, nibbles, and buffets. The second part concentrates on outdoor cooking, with useful tips about the best equipment and ensuring safety, with four chapters full of sizzling barbecue recipes, plus some marvelous salad accompaniments.

Of course, you don't have to confine yourself to just one type of party. Mix and match recipes from different chapters to suit the occasion. For example, you could occupy your guests with a selection of scrumptious dips from the first part of the book, while you get on with grilling one of the delicious marinated dishes from the second. Similarly, all the salads can just as easily be packed into rigid plastic containers for a picnic as they can be served in bowls at a barbecue. They would be a good addition to a buffet table, too.

When entertaining outdoors, the one thing you can't do very far in advance is to take out the food. Not only is it a health risk to leave dishes in hot

sunshine or exposed to flies and other insects, neighborhood cats seem to have an in-built radar for any parties on the block. Once you have taken the food out, put a helpful friend on guard duty. You may, of course, prefer to lay a buffet table indoors with easy access to the yard, but barbecues have to be exclusively alfresco. Make copious use of plastic wrap, cool boxes, and trays of crushed ice. Cool boxes, plastic containers, and screw-top jars for dressings and marinades are essential for picnics and portable barbecues.

Outdoor entertaining is the perfect solution when you have lots of friends with children. For a start, it prevents small feet from treading sausage rolls or chicken drumsticks into your carpets. The occasion tends to be more informal, so the kids are more likely to enjoy themselves, with the result that their parents will, too. If you have the space, why not provide a play corner for very young children with a sandbox? If you can be sure someone will be willing to supervise, you could even fill a baby pool. As far as food is concerned, there are lots of recipes in this book that will appeal to children, from little snacks on skewers to tender homemade burgers.

Mixing and matching recipes is a good idea if you are entertaining both vegetarians and meat-eaters, although each part of the book contains a wide choice of recipes to suit both. In fact, there is something to suit all ages and tastes, from hot and spicy to rich and creamy and from elegant and sophisticated to fresh and fun.

# Party Food

Whether it is a long-planned outdoor celebration or an impromptu alfresco gathering, a party is always a uniquely special occasion. For the host, however, a party may also be a time of stress and hard work. Having to spend time making sure that everyone is mingling, and that the conversation is flowing as freely as the drink, the last thing you need is to be worrying about the food that you are serving. It

should be as much fun to throw a party as it is to attend one. Only you can decide whether your guests will get on with each other or if you can afford to serve champagne, but the first section of this book can at least take away any worries about what snacks to serve to keep your guests happy.

The following section is divided into three chapters, all of which feature vegetarian as well as fish and meat recipes. So, no matter what the tastes of your guests, you can be sure to find dishes here to please everyone. Most of the recipes are for finger foods, which are easy to eat outdoors and will minimize the amount of preparation and clearing up. As well as these, there are a few dishes that simply require a fork to eat them. The emphasis throughout is on tasty treats that are easy to prepare and serve outdoors. After all, you want your guests to enjoy the food but don't want to spend so much time in the kitchen that you are too tired to enjoy yourself.

The chapter on Dips & Pâtés offers a fabulous collection of recipes from around the world which are perfect for easy outdoor entertaining. Delicious treats range from Middle Eastern Baba Ghanoush (see page 26) to Traditional English Potted Shrimp (see page 36). All of these dishes are made in advance and can be laid out in a tempting array with a selection of different breads. Individual recipes provide specific serving suggestions, or you can try some of the party basics on pages 10-11.

Cold Nibbles is the chapter to turn to for the main constituents of your outdoor buffet table. This chapter provides a wide choice of recipes for savory

pastries and cookies; stuffed and pickled vegetables; and tarts and nibbles. There are recipes for traditional favorites, such as Cheese Straws (see page 48) and Sausage Rolls (see page 72). For those with more exotic tastes, there is a selection of exciting and more unusual delicacies. These range from the spicy delight of Deep-Fried Shrimp Balls (see page 64) to the sunny flavor of Stuffed Grape Leaves (see page 68). While all of these snacks are delicious cold, some can also be served warm or hot if you prefer.

The final chapter in this section features a selection of Hot Nibbles. These are always a special treat, but it is easy to be over-ambitious, so the dishes in this book are nice and simple. Many of the recipes can be prepared easily during the party. Others can be prepared in advance, and then popped in the oven or broiled after your guests have arrived.

Whatever kind of outdoor party you are planning, from a family gathering to a 4th July celebration, you will find the best bites and most moreish morsels in this section. You can use the recipes to plan exactly what canapés and snacks will make the best combination for each event. Prepare everything well in advance, and you will be free to enjoy the party as much as your guests.

# Party Basics

Hosting a party, and making some tempting nibbles for your guests, should be fun. All you need is a selection of recipes, and some careful preparation. Don't forget that there are plenty of delicious ready-made nibbles that you can buy to increase the variety of your party snacks and to lessen the time you will need to spend preparing the party food. Plain and flavored breadsticks, corn and tortilla chips, as well as plain potato chips, are great for dunking into homemade dips or just for nibbling on their own. Peanuts are party favorites, but you can also include cashew nuts, almonds, and pistachios. A selection of cheeses and a basket of crackers or crusty bread, served with a dish of butter, is easy and always popular.

If you are already planning to prepare a range of flavorsome foods, you can supplement them with some simpler snacks, such as broiled chicken drumsticks, sausages on sticks, and squares of toast with ready-made toppings such as lumpfish roe (red caviar), sliced hard-cooked eggs, smoked salmon, slices of salami, and soft cheese and chives. Garnish with herb sprigs, sliced stuffed olives, pearl onions, or tiny gherkins. Sandwiches, however, are best avoided as they quickly dry out.

If you don't mind providing cutlery as well as plates, you can also serve a selection of imaginative salads. Most supermarkets sell a wide selection of mixed salad greens and vegetable salads that are ideal for serving at a party. Pasta and rice salads with a colorful mixture of drained canned corn kernels, red and yellow bell pepper strips, tomato wedges, cooked frozen peas, and strips of cooked ham are easily made and can be dressed with vinaigrette or mayonnaise.

## Crudités

Raw and blanched vegetables are perfect for serving with most dips and look very tempting on a large serving platter. Seed and slice red, yellow, or orange bell peppers lengthwise. Baby corn cobs and trimmed, thin asparagus should be blanched in lightly salted boiling water. Include whole cherry tomatoes, small white mushrooms, and trimmed radishes, perhaps with a few small leaves attached. Trim and separate the leaves of red and white chicory or the hearts of young Boston lettuces. Cut raw cauliflower into small florets and slice carrots, celery, and cucumber into sticks.

## Vegetable Chips

Homemade vegetable chips make a delicious alternative to ordinary chips. You can, of course, use potatoes, but you might also like to try parsnips, carrots, or sweet potatoes. Peel the vegetables and slice very thinly using a mandoline or swivel-blade vegetable peeler. Heat corn or peanut oil in a deep-fryer or large pan to 350–375°F/180–190°C, or until a cube of bread browns in 30 seconds. Add the vegetable slices to the oil and fry until golden. Drain on paper towels and sprinkle with sea salt, paprika, or cayenne pepper. Store in an airtight container when cold.

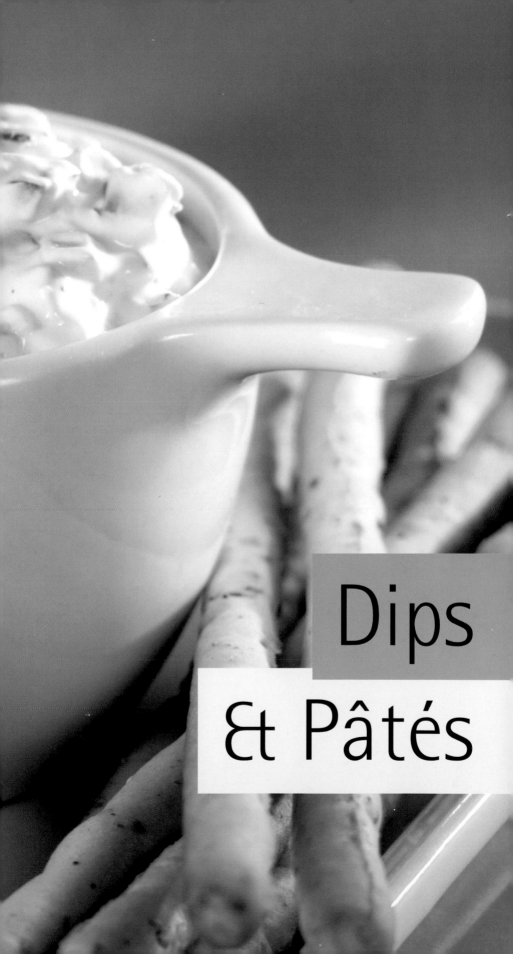

Dips
& Pâtés

# Aïoli

This garlic mayonnaise from the Provence region of France is perfectly partnered with a selection of raw vegetables. It is reputed to keep flies away, so makes the ideal choice for a summer buffet table.

*serves 8*

4 garlic cloves

salt

2 egg yolks

1 cup olive oil

lemon juice

pepper

To serve

crudités (see page 11)

8 hard-cooked eggs, shelled

## Method

❶ Place the garlic cloves and a pinch of salt in a glass bowl and crush with the back of a spoon. Add the egg yolks and beat briefly with an electric mixer until creamy.

❷ Add the oil, a few drops at a time, beating constantly with an electric mixer, until the mixture begins to thicken. Then add the remaining oil in a thin, continuous stream, beating constantly.

❸ Stir in a little lemon juice to give the mayonnaise a dipping consistency. Season to taste with a little more salt, if necessary, and pepper. Cover with plastic wrap and store in the refrigerator until required.

❹ Before serving, return the aïoli to room temperature, if necessary, and transfer to a serving bowl. Arrange the crudités on a large serving platter, arrange the eggs on top, and serve with the aïoli.

# Tzatziki

**This creamy Greek dip is very quick and easy to make, and is wonderfully refreshing on a hot summer's evening.**

## serves 8

1 cucumber

2 garlic cloves

8 scallions

2½ cups strained plain yogurt

5 tbsp chopped fresh mint,

plus extra to garnish

salt and pepper

To serve

toasted mini pita breads

sesame breadsticks

## Method

❶ Trim the cucumber, but do not peel. Cut it into small, neat dice. Finely chop the garlic and scallions.

❷ Beat the yogurt in a bowl with a fork until smooth, then fold in the cucumber, garlic, scallions, and mint. Season to taste with salt and pepper.

❸ Transfer to a serving bowl, cover with plastic wrap, and chill in the refrigerator until required. Garnish with fresh mint and serve with toasted mini pita breads and sesame breadsticks.

# Taramasalata

Homemade taramasalata is infinitely tastier than anything you can buy at a deli, so it is well worth the extra effort. It is traditionally made with gray mullet roe, but cod's roe is easier to find and just as good.

### serves 8

8 oz/225 g (8–10 slices) stale white bread, crusts removed

12 oz/350 g smoked cod's roe

2 garlic cloves, chopped

2 slices onion

4 tbsp lemon juice

¾ cup olive oil

black Kalamata olives, to garnish

chunks of crusty bread, to serve

## Method

❶ Roughly tear up the bread and place it in a bowl. Add cold water to cover and let soak for 10 minutes.

❷ Meanwhile, using a sharp knife, scrape the roe away from the thick outer skin. Place the roe in a food processor with the garlic, onion, and lemon juice. Drain the bread, squeeze out the excess water with your hands, and add it to the food processor. Process the mixture for 2 minutes, or until smooth.

❸ With the motor running, gradually add the oil through the feeder tube until the mixture is smooth and creamy. Scrape into a serving dish, cover with plastic wrap, and chill in the refrigerator until required.

❹ Garnish the taramasalata with the olives. Serve with chunks of crusty bread.

# Guacamole

**It is fortunate that this spicy Mexican dip is so quick to prepare because you cannot make it too far in advance. If you do, the avocados will discolor.**

### *serves 8*

| | |
|---|---|
| 4 avocados | 5 tbsp olive oil |
| 2 garlic cloves | juice of 1½ limes |
| 4 scallions | salt |
| 3 fresh red chiles, seeded | chopped fresh cilantro leaves, to garnish |
| 2 red bell peppers, seeded | tortilla chips, to serve |

## Method

❶ Cut the avocados in half lengthwise and twist the halves to separate. Remove and discard the pits and scoop the flesh into a large bowl with a spoon. Mash coarsely with a fork.

❷ Finely chop the garlic, scallions, chiles, and bell peppers, then stir them into the mashed avocado. Add 4 tablespoons of the oil and the lime juice, season to taste with salt, and stir well to mix. If you prefer a smoother dip, process all the ingredients together in a food processor.

❸ Transfer the guacamole to a serving bowl. Drizzle the remaining oil over the top, sprinkle with the cilantro, and serve with tortilla chips.

# Red Bell Pepper Dip

**Serving this pretty pale-pink dip on a platter of red and white vegetables makes
it look especially appealing—but beware of the spicy kick.**

## *serves 8*

3 red bell peppers, halved and seeded

1 cup cream cheese

½ tsp cayenne pepper

salt

To serve

cherry tomatoes

radishes

radicchio leaves

celery stalks

cauliflower florets

white mushrooms, halved

## Method

❶ Preheat the broiler. Arrange the bell
pepper halves, skin-side up, on a baking
sheet and place under the hot broiler for
10–15 minutes, or until the skins begin to
blacken and blister. Transfer to a plastic
bag with tongs, tie the top, and set aside
until the bell peppers are cool enough
to handle.

❷ Remove the bell peppers from the bag
and peel away the skins. Roughly chop
the flesh and place in a food processor.
Process to a smooth purée, then scrape
into a serving bowl.

❸ Stir in the cream cheese until smooth,
then stir in the cayenne and salt to taste.
Cover with plastic wrap and chill in the
refrigerator until required.

❹ To serve, place the bowl in the center of
a large platter and arrange the tomatoes,
radishes, radicchio, celery, cauliflower, and
mushrooms around it.

# Hummus with Lebanese Seed Bread

Using canned chickpeas in this popular Middle Eastern dip saves time and effort when you are getting party food ready, but you could use dried chickpeas, soaked overnight and cooked in boiling water for about 2½ hours, or until tender.

### *serves 8*

1½ cups canned chickpeas, drained and rinsed

1 cup tahini

4 garlic cloves

juice of 3 lemons

6 tbsp water

salt and pepper

2 tbsp olive oil

**Lebanese seed bread**

½ cup toasted sesame seeds

½ cup poppy seeds

4 tbsp chopped fresh thyme

⅔ cup olive oil

6 pita breads

**To serve**

2 tbsp chopped fresh flatleaf parsley

cayenne pepper

black olives

## Method

❶ Preheat the broiler to medium. For the bread, place the seeds and thyme in a mortar and crush lightly with a pestle. Stir in the oil. Split open the pita breads and brush the seed mixture over the cut sides. Cook under the hot broiler until golden brown and crisp. Let cool. Store in an airtight container until required.

❷ For the hummus place the chickpeas, tahini, garlic, lemon juice, and 4 tablespoons of the water in a food processor. Process until smooth, adding the remaining water if necessary. Alternatively, mash in a bowl with a fork.

❸ Spoon the mixture into a serving dish and season to taste with salt and pepper. Make a shallow hollow in the top of the hummus and spoon in the oil. If you are not serving it immediately, cover with plastic wrap and store in the refrigerator.

❹ Sprinkle the hummus with the parsley, dust lightly with cayenne, and serve with black olives and the Lebanese Seed Bread.

# Baba Ghanoush

**This tasty eggplant dip is not so well known in the West as hummus (see page 24), but is very popular in the Middle East.**

## *serves 8*

3 large eggplants

3 garlic cloves, chopped

6 tbsp tahini

6 tbsp lemon juice

1 tsp ground cumin

3 tbsp chopped fresh flatleaf parsley

salt and pepper

fresh flatleaf parsley sprigs, to garnish

vegetable chips (see page 11), to serve

## Method

❶ Preheat the broiler to low. Prick the eggplants all over with a fork and cut in half lengthwise. Arrange the halves, skin-side up, on a baking sheet and place under the hot broiler for 15 minutes, or until the skins begin to blacken and blister and the flesh feels soft. Remove from the heat and set aside until cool enough to handle.

❷ Peel the eggplants and squeeze out any excess moisture, then roughly chop the flesh and place in a food processor. Add the garlic and 2 tablespoons of the tahini and process to mix, then add 2 tablespoons of the lemon juice and process again. Continue adding the tahini and lemon juice alternately, processing between each addition.

❸ When the mixture is smooth, scrape it into a bowl and stir in the cumin and chopped parsley. Season to taste with salt and pepper.

❹ Transfer the dip to a serving dish. If you are not serving it immediately, cover with plastic wrap and chill in the refrigerator until required. Return the dip to room temperature to serve. Garnish with parsley sprigs and serve with vegetable chips.

# Quick Chicken Liver Pâté with Melba Toast

**Although this is a speedy recipe, you need to leave time for the pâté to cool. If you like, make it up to three days in advance and chill, covered, in the refrigerator.**

*serves 8*

2 tbsp olive oil

2 onions, chopped

2 garlic cloves, finely chopped

1 lb 8 oz/675 g chicken livers

3 tbsp brandy

2 tbsp chopped fresh parsley

1 tbsp chopped fresh sage

salt and pepper

1¼ cups cream cheese

fresh parsley sprigs, to garnish

**Melba toast**

8 slices medium-thick white bread

## Method

❶ Heat the oil in a large, heavy-bottom skillet over low heat. Add the onions and garlic and cook, stirring occasionally, for 5 minutes, until softened.

❷ Add the livers and cook, stirring and turning occasionally, for 5 minutes, or until lightly browned and just beginning to crisp at the edges. Remove the pan from the heat, stir in the brandy, parsley, and sage, and season to taste with salt and pepper. Let cool slightly.

❸ Transfer the mixture to a food processor and process until smooth, scraping down the sides of the bowl once or twice. Scrape the mixture into a bowl, cover with plastic wrap, and let cool completely.

❹ Meanwhile, for the Melba Toast, preheat the broiler to medium; lightly toast the bread on both sides under the hot broiler. Cut off and discard the crusts, then slice each half to make two very thin slices, each with one untoasted side. Toast the uncooked sides of the bread until lightly golden and the edges begin to curl slightly. Remove from the broiler and let cool. When completely cool, store in an airtight container until required.

❺ When the chicken liver mixture is cold, stir in the cream cheese and mix well. Cover with plastic wrap and chill in the refrigerator until required. Return to room temperature to serve. Garnish with parsley sprigs and serve with the Melba Toast.

# Smoked Fish Pâté

Kippered herring fillets are used here because they have such a rich flavor when they have been hot smoked in the traditional way. You could also use whitefish or smoked mackerel, in which case omit the preliminary cooking in Step 1.

### serves 8

2 lb/900 g undyed kippered herring fillets

2 garlic cloves, finely chopped

¾ cups olive oil

6 tbsp light cream

salt and pepper

lemon slices, to garnish

crackers, to serve

## Method

❶ Place the kippers in a large skillet or fish kettle and add cold water to just cover. Bring to a boil, then immediately reduce the heat and poach gently for 10 minutes, until tender. If using a skillet, you may need to do this in batches.

❷ Transfer the fish to a cutting board using a fish slice. Remove and discard the skin. Roughly flake the flesh with a fork and remove any remaining tiny bones. Transfer the fish to a pan and add the garlic. Place over low heat and break up the fish with a wooden spoon.

❸ Gradually add the olive oil, beating well after each addition. Add the cream and beat until smooth, but do not allow the mixture to boil.

❹ Remove the pan from the heat and season to taste with salt, if necessary, and pepper. Spoon the pâté into a serving dish, cover, and let cool completely. Chill in the refrigerator until required (it can be refrigerated for up to 3 days).

❺ Garnish with lemon slices and serve with crackers.

# Mushroom &
# Chestnut Pâté

This is a gloriously luxurious vegetarian party treat. Dried porcini are quite
expensive, but they have a wonderfully intense flavor and you don't need many.

## serves 8

8 oz/225 g dried chestnuts,
soaked overnight

1 oz/25 g dried porcini mushrooms

4 tbsp hot water

4 tbsp Marsala or medium sherry

1 tbsp olive oil

1 lb 8 oz/675 g cremini or portabello
mushrooms, sliced

1 tbsp balsamic vinegar

1 tbsp chopped fresh parsley

1 tbsp soy sauce

salt and pepper

thinly sliced radish, to garnish

whole-wheat toast triangles or
crusty bread, to serve

## Method

❶ Drain the chestnuts, place them in a pan, and add cold water to cover. Bring to a boil, then reduce the heat, cover, and simmer for 45 minutes until tender. Drain.

❷ Meanwhile, place the porcini in a small bowl with the hot water and 1 tablespoon of the Marsala. Let soak for 20 minutes. Drain well, reserving the soaking liquid. Pat the mushrooms dry with paper towels. Strain the soaking liquid through a chinois or coffee filter paper.

❸ Heat the oil in a large, heavy-based skillet. Add the cremini mushrooms and cook over low heat, stirring occasionally, for 5 minutes, until softened.

❹ Add the porcini, the soaking liquid, and vinegar, and cook, stirring constantly, for 1 minute. Increase the heat and stir in the remaining Marsala. Cook, stirring frequently, for 3 minutes. Remove from the heat.

❺ Transfer the chestnuts to a food processor and process to a purée. Add the mushroom mixture and parsley and process to a smooth paste. Add the soy sauce and salt and pepper to taste and briefly process again to mix.

❻ Scrape the pâté into a serving bowl, cover, and chill in the refrigerator. Garnish with radish slices before serving and serve with toast triangles or crusty bread.

# Cheese & Bean Pâté

This creamy pâté is based on classic Italian ingredients—ricotta and borlotti or cannellini beans, flavored with garlic, lemon juice, and flatleaf parsley.

*serves 8*

1 lb 12 oz/800 g canned borlotti or cannellini beans, drained and rinsed

1½ cups ricotta cheese

2 garlic cloves, coarsely chopped

4 tbsp lemon juice

½ cup butter, melted

3 tbsp chopped fresh flatleaf parsley

salt and pepper

corn oil, for greasing

cheese-flavored focaccia fingers, to serve

To garnish

fresh flatleaf parsley sprigs

lemon wedges

## Method

❶ Place the beans, ricotta, garlic, lemon juice, and melted butter in a food processor and process to a smooth purée. Add the chopped parsley and salt and pepper to taste and process again briefly to mix.

❷ Lightly oil a plain ring mold. Scrape the mixture into the mold and smooth the surface. Cover with plastic wrap and chill in the refrigerator until set.

❸ To serve, turn out the pâté on to a serving dish and fill the center with parsley sprigs. Garnish with lemon wedges and serve with focaccia fingers.

# Traditional English Potted Shrimp

For authenticity, potted shrimp should be served with brown bread spread with unsalted butter, but you could also serve them with whole-wheat toast, Melba Toast (see page 28), or even chunks of soda bread.

*serves 8*

1¼ cups unsalted butter

3 pieces mace blade

pinch of freshly grated nutmeg

pinch of cayenne pepper

1 lb/450 g cooked, shelled tiny shrimp

slices of brown bread, spread with
unsalted butter, to serve

To garnish

fresh parsley sprigs

lemon slices

## Method

❶ Place ¾ cup of the butter in a small, heavy-bottom pan and add the mace, nutmeg, and cayenne. Melt over the lowest possible heat, stirring occasionally.

❷ Add the shrimp and cook, stirring constantly, for 2 minutes, or until heated through. Do not allow the mixture to boil.

❸ Remove the pan from the heat, then remove and discard the mace. Spoon the mixture into a serving dish and level the surface. Cover and let cool, then chill in the refrigerator until set. (Traditionally, they are served in ramekins as individual appetizers. If you want to do this, divide the mixture between 8 ramekin dishes.)

❹ When the potted shrimp have set, place the remaining butter in a small, heavy-bottom pan. Melt over low heat, then skim off the scum that has formed on the surface. Carefully pour off the clear liquid into a bowl, leaving the white milk solids in the base of the pan. Spoon the clarified butter over the top of the potted shrimp to make a thin, covering layer. Cover and return to the refrigerator until set.

❺ Garnish the potted shrimp with parsley sprigs and lemon slices and serve with the buttered slices of bread.

Cold

Nibbles

# Three-Flavor Pinwheels

**These tasty little morsels look so appetizing that your guests are sure to snap them up.**

*makes 50–60*

Ham & cream cheese pinwheels

¾ cup cream cheese

4 large slices cooked lean ham

4 tbsp snipped fresh chives


Beef & horseradish pinwheels

½ cup heavy cream

2 tbsp creamed horseradish

4 large slices medium-rare roast beef

Smoked salmon & dill cream pinwheels

1 cup heavy cream

2 tbsp chopped fresh dill

pepper

4 large or 8 medium slices smoked salmon

4 tbsp lemon juice

## Method

❶ For the Ham & Cream Cheese Pinwheels, spread the cream cheese evenly over the slices of ham. Sprinkle with the chives. Roll up each slice tightly and wrap individually in plastic wrap. Let chill in the refrigerator for 1 hour.

❷ For the Beef & Horseradish Pinwheels, whip the cream in a bowl until stiff, then fold in the creamed horseradish. Spread the mixture evenly over the slices of beef. Roll up each slice tightly and wrap individually in plastic wrap. Let chill in the refrigerator for 1 hour.

❸ For the Smoked Salmon & Dill Cream Pinwheels, whip the cream in a bowl until stiff, then fold in the dill and pepper to taste. Spread the mixture evenly over the slices of smoked salmon. Roll up each slice tightly and wrap individually in plastic wrap. Chill in the refrigerator for 1 hour.

❹ When ready to serve, unwrap the rolls one at a time and thinly slice. Before slicing the Smoked Salmon & Dill Cream Pinwheels, sprinkle with a little lemon juice. Impale each pinwheel on a wooden toothpick and arrange on a serving platter.

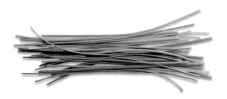

# Egg & Tapenade Toasties

Tapenade is a black olive, caper, and anchovy paste from Provence. It goes especially well with hard-cooked eggs, but you could also top these toasties with flaked canned tuna.

### *makes 8*

| | |
|---|---|
| 1 small French loaf | **Tapenade** |
| 4 tomatoes, thinly sliced | 1 cup chopped black olives |
| 4 eggs, hard-cooked | 6 bottled or canned anchovy fillets |
| 4 bottled or canned anchovy fillets in | in olive oil, drained |
| olive oil, drained and halved lengthwise | 2 tbsp capers, rinsed |
| 8 marinated pitted black olives | 2 garlic cloves, roughly chopped |
| | 1 tsp Dijon mustard |
| | 2 tbsp lemon juice |
| | 1 tsp fresh thyme leaves |
| | pepper |
| | 4–5 tbsp olive oil |

# Method

❶ For the Tapenade, place the olives, anchovies, capers, garlic, mustard, lemon juice, thyme, and pepper to taste in a food processor and process for 20–25 seconds, or until smooth. Scrape down the sides of the mixing bowl, then with the motor running, gradually add the oil through the feeder tube to make a smooth paste. Spoon the paste into a bowl, cover with plastic wrap, and reserve until required.

❷ Preheat the broiler. Cut the French loaf into 8 slices, discarding the crusty ends.

Toast on both sides under the hot broiler until light golden brown. Let cool.

❸ To assemble the toasties, spread a little of the tapenade on one side of each slice of toast. Top with the tomato slices. Shell the eggs, then slice and arrange over the tomatoes. Dot a little of the remaining tapenade on each egg slice. Wind the anchovy fillets on top of the egg slices in an "S" shape. Halve the marinated olives, arrange 2 halves on each toasty, and serve.

# Filled Croustades

Much more fun than sandwiches—and less likely to become dry and unappetizing—
these crisp containers go well with an endless variety of easy-to-make fillings.
In addition to those below, scrambled eggs topped with slivers of ham or salami
and cucumber; Smoked Fish Pâté (see page 30), garnished with sliced stuffed
olives; or Guacamole (see page 20), topped with chopped tomato and pickled
jalapeño chiles, would work well.

## *makes 48*

| Croustades | Crab salad filling |
|---|---|
| 1 lb 5 oz/600 g butter | 4 oz/115 g crabmeat, drained if canned |
| 12 large slices white bread | and thawed if frozen |
| | ½ cup mayonnaise |
| **Cheese & tomato filling** | pinch of celery salt |
| Tapenade (see page 42) | 2 eggs, hard-cooked |
| mozzarella cheese, thinly sliced | fresh dill sprigs, to garnish |
| cherry tomatoes, halved | |
| fresh basil leaves, to garnish | |

## Method

❶ Preheat the oven to 350°F/180°C. Make the Croustades in 4 batches. Melt one-quarter of the butter in a heavy-bottom pan over low heat. Meanwhile, stamp out 12 rounds of bread with a 3-inch/7.5-cm fluted cookie cutter. When the butter has melted, remove the pan from the heat. Dip the bread rounds into the butter and press them firmly into the cups of a muffin pan.

❷ Place a second muffin pan on top to keep the bread rounds in shape. Bake in the preheated oven for 15–20 minutes, or until the Croustades are crisp and firm. Transfer to a wire rack to cool completely while you cook the remaining batches. When the croustades are cold, fill with your chosen filling and serve.

❸ For the Cheese & Tomato Filling, spoon Tapenade into the Croustades, top each one with a slice of mozzarella and a tomato half, and garnish with a basil leaf.

❹ For the Crab Salad Filling, place the crabmeat in a bowl and flake with a fork. Stir in the mayonnaise and celery salt. Shell the eggs, finely chop, and stir into the filling mixture. Spoon into the Croustades and garnish with dill sprigs.

# Easy Nibbles

Lots of different flavors and textures, and food that is easy to handle and eat, are the keys to party success. This duo of tasty treats satisfies all those criteria.

## *makes 40*

| Celery & endive boats | Deviled eggs |
|---|---|
| 2 cups cream cheese | 6 hard-cooked eggs, shelled |
| 4 scallions, finely chopped | 2 scallions, finely chopped |
| 4 tbsp chopped sun-dried tomatoes in oil | 6 walnut halves, finely chopped |
| 3 tbsp chopped fresh parsley | 1 tbsp mayonnaise |
| 1 tbsp snipped fresh chives | 2 fresh green chiles, seeded and |
| 1 cup chopped pimiento-stuffed olives | finely chopped |
| 1 tbsp Tabasco sauce | 1 tbsp Dijon mustard |
| 2 heads Belgian endive, separated | 1 tsp white wine vinegar |
| into leaves | cayenne pepper |
| 12 celery stalks | salt and pepper |
| fine strips of red bell pepper, to garnish | thinly sliced baby gherkins, to garnish |

## Method

❶ For the Celery & Endive Boats, beat the cream cheese in a bowl with a wooden spoon until smooth. Stir in the scallions, sun-dried tomatoes, parsley, chives, olives, and Tabasco and mix well. Spoon the mixture into the hollows of the Belgian endive leaves and celery stalks and arrange on a serving plate. Garnish with the strips of red bell pepper.

❷ For the Deviled Eggs, cut the eggs in half lengthwise and scoop out the yolks into a bowl without piercing the whites. Mash the yolks well with a fork, then mix in the scallions, walnuts, mayonnaise, chiles, mustard, and vinegar. Season to taste with cayenne, salt, and pepper. Spoon the mixture into the egg white halves and garnish with gherkin slices.

# Cheese Straws

**Nothing could be simpler or more popular than freshly made cheese straws. You can make the dough in advance, bake one batch, and store the remainder, wrapped in foil in the refrigerator, to bake during the party and replenish supplies.**

## *makes 60*

| | |
|---|---|
| scant 2 cups all-purpose flour, plus extra for dusting | ¾ cup freshly grated Parmesan or romano cheese |
| salt and pepper | 2 egg yolks |
| cayenne pepper | 1–2 tbsp cold water (optional) |
| mustard powder | 1 egg white, lightly beaten, to glaze |
| ½ cup butter, diced, plus extra for greasing | |

## Method

❶ Preheat the oven to 425°F/220°C. Sift the flour into a bowl with a pinch each of salt, pepper, cayenne, and mustard powder. Add the butter and rub it in with your fingertips until the mixture resembles bread crumbs. Stir in the cheese. Add the egg yolks and mix well, adding a little of the cold water, as required, to bind. Shape the dough into a ball.

❷ Grease several cookie sheets. Roll out the dough on a lightly floured counter to about ½ inch/1 cm thick. Using a sharp knife, cut it into fingers and arrange on the cookie sheets, spaced slightly apart. Brush with the egg white.

❸ Bake in the preheated oven for 8–10 minutes, or until golden brown. Remove from the oven and let cool on the cookie sheets. When completely cool, store in an airtight container, but they are best served as fresh as possible.

# Quiche Lorraine

This elegant version of the classic French egg and bacon tart is delicious as it is, or can form the basis of an even more elaborate quiche. You can, for example, arrange cooked or canned asparagus spears in a wheel on the top, or smother it with a layer of lightly sautéed mushrooms.

*makes 1 x 9-inch/23-cm quiche*

### Pastry

scant 1½ cups all-purpose flour, plus extra for dusting

pinch of salt

½ cup butter, diced

¼ cup freshly grated romano cheese

4–6 tbsp ice water

### Filling

1 cup thinly sliced Gruyère cheese

½ cup crumbled Roquefort cheese

6 oz/175 g rindless lean bacon, broiled until crisp

3 eggs

⅔ cup heavy cream

salt and pepper

## Method

❶ To make the pastry, sift the flour with the salt into a bowl. Add the butter and rub it in with your fingertips until the mixture resembles bread crumbs. Stir in the grated cheese, then stir in enough of the water to bind. Shape the dough into a ball, wrap in foil, and chill in the refrigerator for 15 minutes.

❷ Preheat the oven to 375°F/190°C. Unwrap and roll out the dough on a lightly floured counter. Use to line a 9-inch/23-cm quiche pan. Place the pan on a cookie sheet. Prick the base of the pastry shell all over with a fork, line with foil or parchment paper, and fill with pie weights. Bake in the preheated oven for 15 minutes until the edges are set and dry. Remove the pie weights and lining and bake the pastry shell for a further 5–7 minutes, or until golden. Let cool slightly.

❸ For the filling, arrange both cheeses over the base of the pastry shell. Crumble the bacon evenly on top. In a bowl, beat the eggs with the cream until thoroughly combined. Add salt and pepper to taste. Pour the mixture into the pastry shell and return to the oven for 20 minutes, or until the filling is golden and set.

❹ Remove from the oven and cool the quiche in the pan for 10 minutes. Transfer to a wire rack to cool completely. Cover and store in the refrigerator, but return to room temperature before serving.

# Moroccan Pickled Vegetables

**Snacking is an art form in North Africa, so it is well worth adopting their clever ideas to serve as flavorful party food.**

*serves 12*

24 small radishes

24 baby carrots

8 celery stalks

1 cucumber

salt and pepper

$\frac{1}{2}$ cup superfine sugar

$\frac{1}{2}$ cup lemon juice

2 tbsp pink peppercorns

1 bunch of fresh cilantro, finely chopped

## Method

❶ Place the radishes and carrots in a large, nonmetallic bowl. Cut the celery stalks into 2-inch/5-cm lengths and add to the bowl. Halve the cucumber lengthwise, scoop out the seeds with a teaspoon and discard, then thickly slice and add to the bowl. Sprinkle the vegetables generously with salt, cover with plastic wrap, and let stand for 3–4 hours.

❷ Tip the vegetables into a colander and rinse thoroughly under cold running water to remove all traces of salt. Drain well and pat dry with paper towels. Transfer the vegetables to a nonmetallic bowl.

❸ In a separate nonmetallic bowl, mix together the sugar, lemon juice, and peppercorns, stirring until the sugar has completely dissolved. Season to taste with pepper.

❹ Pour the dressing over the vegetables and toss gently to mix. Cover with plastic wrap and chill for 8 hours or overnight in the refrigerator.

❺ Just before serving, stir in the chopped cilantro, then transfer to a serving dish. Serve chilled with a supply of wooden toothpicks for spearing the vegetables.

# Böreks

These crisp, cheese-filled pastries are a Turkish specialty, although they are popular throughout the Middle East. They are traditionally made with sheep's milk cheese, but you could substitute grated Gruyère if you prefer.

## makes 20

8 oz/225 g feta cheese (drained weight)

2 tbsp chopped fresh mint

2 tbsp chopped fresh parsley

1½ tbsp chopped fresh dill

pinch of freshly grated nutmeg

pepper

20 sheets phyllo pastry

(about 4½ x 7 inches/12 x 18 cm),

thawed if frozen

olive oil, for brushing

# Method

❶ Preheat the oven to 375°F/190°C. Crumble the feta into a bowl and add the mint, parsley, dill, and nutmeg. Season to taste with pepper and mix thoroughly.

❷ Keep the phyllo pastry sheets covered with plastic wrap to prevent them drying out. Take a sheet of phyllo and brush with oil. Place a second sheet on top and brush with oil. Cut in half lengthwise. Place a teaspoon of the cheese mixture at the short end of one long strip, fold in the corners diagonally, and roll up. Brush the end with a little oil to seal and place, seam-side down, on a cookie sheet. Repeat with the remaining sheets of phyllo and filling.

❸ Brush the tops of the pastries with a little more oil and bake in the preheated oven for 15–20 minutes, or until golden and crisp. Remove from the oven and transfer to a wire rack to cool. Serve at room temperature. The böreks can also be deep-fried.

# Little Feta & Spinach Crescents

The traditional recipe for spanakopita, a famous Greek pie, has been adapted to make these attractive, melt-in-the mouth crescents.

## makes 16

1 lb/450 g spinach, thick stalks removed

4 scallions, finely chopped

2 eggs, lightly beaten

1 tbsp chopped fresh parsley

1 tbsp chopped fresh dill

12 oz/350 g feta cheese (drained weight)

pepper

8 sheets phyllo pastry (about 4½ x 7 inches/ 12 x 18 cm), thawed if frozen

olive oil, for brushing

## Method

**❶** Preheat the oven to 375°F/190°C. Pour water to a depth of about ½ inch/ 1 cm into a large pan and bring to a boil. Add the spinach and cook, turning once, for 1–2 minutes, or until just wilted. Drain well, then squeeze out as much excess liquid as you can with your hands. Finely chop the spinach and place in a large bowl. Add the scallions, eggs, parsley, and dill. Crumble in the feta cheese and season to taste with pepper. Mix together thoroughly.

**❷** Keep the phyllo pastry sheets covered with plastic wrap to prevent them drying out. Take a sheet of phyllo, brush with oil, and cut in half lengthwise. Spread a little of the filling across one corner, leaving a small margin on either side. Roll up securely but not too tightly and curl in the ends to make a crescent shape. Place on a cookie sheet. Repeat with the remaining sheets of phyllo and filling.

**❸** Brush the crescents with oil and bake in the preheated oven for 25 minutes, until golden and crisp. Remove from the oven and let stand on the cookie sheet for 5 minutes, then transfer to a wire rack to cool. Serve at room temperature.

# Cheese & Apricot Morsels

**These unusual little snacks make an eye-catching addition to a buffet table, yet are very easy and quick to make.**

## *makes 20*

1 cup cream cheese

6 tbsp milk

1 cup finely grated sharp Cheddar cheese

salt and pepper

1 lb 12 oz/800 g apricot halves,
drained if canned

To garnish

about 20 walnut pieces

paprika

## Method

❶ Beat the cream cheese in a bowl with a wooden spoon until softened. Gradually beat in the milk and Cheddar cheese. Season to taste with salt and pepper.

❷ Spoon the cheese mixture into a pastry bag fitted with a ½-inch/1-cm star tip. Pipe swirls of the mixture into the hollow side of each apricot half.

❸ Arrange the filled apricot halves in a serving dish, then top each with a piece of walnut and dust lightly with a little paprika to garnish.

# Caribbean Crab Cakes

These spicy snacks are delicious served warm as well as cold and go well with the Red Bell Pepper Dip (see page 22) or Spicy Salsa (see page 78).

## *makes 16*

1 potato, cut into chunks

pinch of salt

4 scallions, chopped

1 garlic clove, chopped

1 tbsp chopped fresh thyme

1 tbsp chopped fresh basil

1 tbsp chopped fresh cilantro

8 oz/225 g white crabmeat, drained if canned and thawed if frozen

½ tsp Dijon mustard

½ fresh green chile, seeded and finely chopped

1 egg, lightly beaten

pepper

all-purpose flour, for dusting

corn oil, for frying

lime wedges, to garnish

dip or salsa of choice, to serve

## Method

❶ Place the potato in a small pan and add water to cover. Add the salt. Bring to a boil, then reduce the heat, cover, and simmer for 10–15 minutes, or until softened. Drain well, turn into a large bowl, and mash with a potato masher or fork until smooth.

❷ Meanwhile, place the scallions, garlic, thyme, basil, and cilantro in a mortar and pound with a pestle until smooth. Add the herb paste to the mashed potato with the crabmeat, mustard, chile, egg, and pepper to taste. Mix well, cover with plastic wrap, and chill in the refrigerator for 30 minutes.

❸ Sprinkle flour on to a shallow plate. Shape spoonfuls of the crabmeat mixture into small balls with your hands, then flatten slightly and dust with flour, shaking off any excess. Heat the oil in a skillet over high heat, add the crab cakes, in batches, and cook for 2–3 minutes on each side until golden. Remove from the pan and drain on paper towels. Let cool to room temperature.

❹ Arrange the crab cakes on a serving dish and garnish with lime wedges. Serve with a bowl of dip or salsa.

# Anchovy, Olive &
# Cheese Triangles

Ideal for parties, these fabulous little Spanish tapas can be made in advance
and stored in an airtight container. If you can't find Manchego cheese,
substitute sharp Cheddar.

*makes 40*

2 oz/55 g canned anchovy fillets in olive
oil, drained and roughly chopped
½ cup roughly chopped
pitted black olives
1 cup finely grated Manchego cheese

scant 1 cup all-purpose flour,
plus extra for dusting
½ cup unsalted butter, diced
½ tsp cayenne pepper,
plus extra for dusting

## Method

❶ Place the anchovies, olives, cheese,
flour, butter, and cayenne in a food
processor and pulse until a dough forms.
Turn out and shape into a ball. Wrap in foil
and chill in the refrigerator for 30 minutes.

❷ Preheat the oven to 400°F/200°C.
Unwrap the dough, knead on a lightly
floured counter, and roll out thinly. Using
a sharp knife, cut it into strips about
2 inches/5 cm wide. Cut diagonally across
each strip, turning the knife in alternate
directions, to make triangles.

❸ Arrange the triangles on 2 cookie sheets
and dust lightly with cayenne. Bake in the
preheated oven for 10 minutes, or until
golden brown. Transfer to wire racks to
cool completely.

# Deep-Fried Shrimp Balls

These spicy Indonesian snacks are very moreish and are delicious served hot or cold. Sambal oelek is a fiery hot paste made from chiles. It is available from large supermarkets and Asian food stores.

## *makes 25*

10 oz/280 g raw shrimp, shelled and deveined

1-inch/2.5-cm piece fresh gingerroot, roughly chopped

2½ cups bean sprouts, roughly chopped

1 bunch of scallions, roughly chopped

scant 1 cup all-purpose flour

1 tsp baking powder

1 egg, lightly beaten

½ tsp sambal oelek

pinch of salt

1–2 tbsp lukewarm water (optional)

peanut or corn oil, for deep-frying

dip of choice, to serve (optional)

## Method

❶ Place the shrimp, ginger, bean sprouts, and scallions in a food processor and process until finely chopped, scraping down the sides of the mixing bowl once or twice. Scrape the mixture into a bowl and add the flour, baking powder, egg, sambal oelek, and salt. Mix thoroughly with your hands until a firm mixture forms, adding a little of the water if necessary.

❷ Heat the oil in a deep-fryer or large pan to 350–375°F/180–190°C, or until a cube of bread browns in 30 seconds.

❸ Meanwhile, shape spoonfuls of the shrimp mixture into walnut-size balls with your hands. Add the shrimp balls to the hot oil, in batches, and deep-fry for 2–3 minutes, or until golden brown. Remove with a slotted spoon and drain on paper towels. Let cool to room temperature before serving with a dip, if desired. Alternatively, serve hot immediately after the shrimp balls are drained, with a dip, if desired.

# Sicilian Shrimp

**This attractive dish makes a lovely centerpiece for a buffet table, but you will need to provide plates and forks for your guests.**

## serves 12

2¾ cups long-grain rice

3 tbsp white wine vinegar

1 tsp Dijon mustard

2 garlic cloves

⅔ cup olive oil

salt and pepper

paprika

1¾ cups mayonnaise

juice of 3 oranges

juice of ½ lemon

3 shallots, finely chopped

2 cups strained tomatoes

1 lb/450 g cooked, shelled shrimp

1 cup slivered almonds

corn oil, for greasing

fresh parsley sprigs, to garnish

## Method

❶ Bring a large pan of lightly salted water to a boil. Add the rice and return to a boil. Reduce the heat and simmer for 15 minutes, or until tender. Drain well, rinse under cold running water, then drain again and let cool completely.

❷ Mix the vinegar and mustard together in a nonmetallic bowl. Place the garlic on a cutting board and smash with the side of a large, heavy knife. Sprinkle over a little salt and finely chop. Add the garlic to the vinegar mixture and mix, then gradually whisk in the oil until the dressing has thickened. Add salt and pepper to taste and lightly color with paprika. Reserve.

❸ Mix the mayonnaise, orange juice, lemon juice, shallots, and tomatoes together in a separate, nonmetallic bowl. Fold in the shrimp. Cover with plastic wrap and chill in the refrigerator until required.

❹ When the rice is cold, add the dressing and stir in the almonds. Spoon the rice mixture into a lightly oiled round mold, cover with plastic wrap, and chill in the refrigerator for at least 30 minutes.

❺ To serve, turn out the rice on to a large serving plate, carefully scoop out the center, and spoon the shrimp mixture into the hollow. Garnish with parsley sprigs.

# Stuffed Grape Leaves

**With all the sunny flavors of Greece, these vegetarian parcels are perfect for a summer party.**

*serves 12*

2 cups long-grain rice

1 lb/450 g grape leaves, rinsed if preserved in brine

2 onions, finely chopped

1 bunch of scallions, finely chopped

1 bunch of fresh parsley, finely chopped

½ cup finely chopped fresh mint

1 tbsp fennel seeds

1 tsp crushed dried chiles

finely grated rind of 2 lemons

1 cup olive oil

salt

2½ cups boiling water

lemon wedges, to garnish

Tzatziki (see page 16), to serve

# Method

❶ Bring a large pan of lightly salted water to a boil. Add the rice and return to a boil. Reduce the heat and simmer for 15 minutes, or until tender.

❷ Meanwhile, if using preserved grape leaves, place them in a heatproof bowl and pour over boiling water to cover. Let soak for 10 minutes. If using fresh grape leaves, bring a pan of water to a boil, add the grape leaves, then reduce the heat and simmer for 10 minutes.

❸ Drain the rice and mix with the onions, scallions, parsley, mint, fennel seeds, chiles, lemon rind, and 3 tablespoons of the oil in a large bowl. Season to taste with salt.

❹ Drain the grape leaves well. Spread out 1 leaf, vein-side up, on a counter. Place a generous teaspoonful of the rice mixture on the leaf near the stalk. Fold the stalk end over the filling, fold in the sides, and roll up the leaf. Repeat until all the filling has been used. Use any leftover grape leaves to line a serving platter, if desired.

❺ Place the parcels in a large, heavy-bottom pan in a single layer (you may need to use 2 pans). Spoon over the remaining oil, then add the boiling water. Cover the parcels with an inverted heatproof plate to keep them below the surface of the water, cover the pan, and simmer for 1 hour.

❻ Let the parcels cool to room temperature in the pan, then transfer to a serving platter with a slotted spoon. Garnish with lemon wedges and serve with Tzatziki.

# Vegetable Samosas

These aromatic Indian snacks are always popular and taste good served hot or cold. You can make them in advance and freeze them ready to cook or to serve after thawing.

*makes 30*

3 large potatoes, cut into chunks

salt

¾ cup frozen peas

½ cup frozen corn kernels, thawed

2 shallots, finely chopped

1 tsp ground cumin

1 tsp ground coriander

2 fresh green chiles, seeded and finely chopped

2 tbsp chopped fresh mint

2 tbsp chopped fresh cilantro

4 tbsp lemon juice

15 sheets phyllo pastry (about 4½ x 7 inches/12 x 18 cm), thawed if frozen

melted butter, for brushing

peanut or corn oil, for deep-frying

mango chutney, to serve

## Method

❶ Place the potatoes in a pan and add cold water to cover and a pinch of salt. Bring to a boil, then reduce the heat, cover, and simmer for 15–20 minutes, or until tender. Meanwhile, cook the peas according to the instructions on the package. Drain and transfer to a bowl. Drain the potatoes, return to the pan, and mash coarsely with a potato masher or fork. Add them to the peas.

❷ Add the corn, shallots, cumin, coriander, chiles, mint, cilantro, lemon juice, and salt to taste. Mix well.

❸ Keep the phyllo pastry sheets covered with plastic wrap to prevent them drying out. Take a sheet of phyllo pastry, brush with melted butter, and cut in half lengthwise. Place a tablespoonful of the filling at one end of a strip. Fold over a corner to make a triangle and roll up the pastry strip. Repeat with the remaining sheets of phyllo and filling.

❹ Heat the oil in a deep-fryer or large pan to 350–375°F/180–190°C, or until a cube of bread browns in 30 seconds. Cook the samosas, in batches, until golden brown. Remove with a slotted spoon and drain on kitchen paper. Alternatively, bake in a preheated oven at 400°F/200°C for 10–15 minutes, until golden brown. Serve at room temperature with mango chutney.

# Sausage Rolls

**Homemade sausage rolls are so much tastier than the store-bought variety, especially if you can buy good-quality ground pork. They are very easy to make and can be served warm or cold.**

*makes 48*

1 lb/450 g ground pork

1 tsp Worcestershire sauce

beaten egg, to glaze

**Pastry**

scant 2 cups all-purpose flour, plus extra for dusting

pinch of salt

½ tsp mustard powder

½ cup butter, diced

2–3 tbsp ice water

## Method

❶ For the pastry, sift the flour into a bowl with the salt and mustard powder. Add the butter and rub it in with your fingertips until the mixture resembles bread crumbs. Gradually stir in enough of the water to make a soft, but not sticky, dough. Shape the dough into a ball, wrap in foil, and chill in the refrigerator for 20 minutes.

❷ Preheat the oven to 375°F/190°C. Mix together the pork and Worcestershire sauce in a bowl until thoroughly combined and the meat is broken up. Divide the mixture into 12 portions and roll each one between the palms of your hands to make a 6-inch/15-cm long sausage.

❸ Roll out the dough on a lightly floured counter to a rectangle measuring 8 x 18 inches/20 x 46 cm. Using a sharp knife, cut the dough into 12 rectangles, each measuring about 2 x 6 inches/ 5 x 15 cm. Place a pork roll on a dough rectangle and brush the long edges of the dough with water. Carefully roll the pastry over the meat to enclose it, then cut the roll into 4 equal pieces. Repeat with the remaining dough and pork rolls.

❹ Arrange the sausage rolls on 2 cookie sheets, seam-side down. Brush with the beaten egg and bake in the preheated oven for 10 minutes, or until golden brown and cooked through. Remove from the oven and transfer the sausage rolls to a wire rack to cool.

# Honey & Mustard Drumsticks

**Chicken drumsticks make good party food as they are so easy to eat with the fingers. This sweet and sour marinade makes them completely irresistible.**

## *makes 12*

12 chicken drumsticks

6 tbsp clear honey

6 tbsp whole-grain mustard

2 tbsp Dijon mustard

2 tbsp white wine vinegar

3 tbsp corn oil

fresh parsley sprigs, to garnish

## Method

❶ Using a sharp knife, make several slashes in each drumstick, then place them in a large, nonmetallic dish.

❷ Mix the honey, both types of mustard, vinegar, and oil together in a pitcher, whisking well to combine. Pour the marinade over the chicken, turning and stirring to coat. Cover with plastic wrap and let marinate in the refrigerator for at least 2–3 hours or overnight.

❸ Preheat the broiler to medium. Drain the chicken drumsticks, reserving the marinade. Place the drumsticks on a broiler rack and cook under the hot broiler, turning and brushing frequently with the marinade, for 25 minutes, or until the chicken is tender and the juices run clear when a skewer is inserted into the thickest part of the meat. Let cool, then arrange the drumsticks on a serving platter and garnish with parsley sprigs.

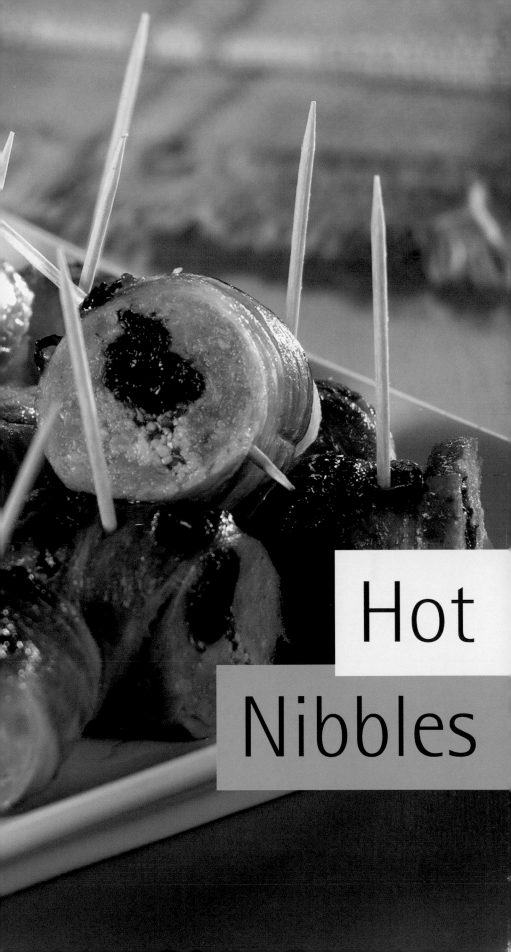

Hot
Nibbles

# Spicy Seafood Kabobs

**These tempting shrimp and angler fish skewers are perfect for parties because they take only a few minutes to cook.**

*makes 8*

2 tsp grated fresh gingerroot

2 garlic cloves, finely chopped

2 fresh green chiles, seeded and finely chopped

2 tbsp peanut or corn oil

3 lb 5 oz/1.5 kg angler fish fillet, cut into 24 chunks

8 raw jumbo shrimp, shelled and tails left intact

salt and pepper

Spicy salsa

2 tomatoes

4 fresh Scotch bonnet chiles

4 fresh green jalapeño chiles, seeded and finely chopped

2 tbsp chopped fresh cilantro

2 tbsp olive oil

1 tbsp red wine vinegar

## Method

❶ Mix the ginger, garlic, green chiles, and peanut oil together in a large, nonmetallic bowl. Add the angler fish chunks and shrimp and stir well to coat. Cover with plastic wrap and let marinate in the refrigerator for 1 hour.

❷ Preheat the broiler to medium. To make the salsa, cut a cross in the bottom of each tomato, place in a heatproof bowl, and pour over boiling water to cover. Let stand for 30 seconds. Drain, let cool, then peel.

❸ Place the Scotch bonnet chiles on a cookie sheet and cook under the broiler, turning frequently, until the skin blackens and blisters. Using tongs, transfer to a plastic bag and tie the top.

❹ Place the jalapeño chiles in a bowl. Scoop out and discard the tomato seeds, finely chop the flesh, and add to the bowl. Remove the Scotch bonnet chiles from the bag and peel away the skins. Halve them, discard the seeds, and finely chop the flesh. (Wear rubber gloves to protect your hands as they are very hot.) Add them to the bowl with the cilantro. Whisk the oil with the vinegar in a small bowl and season to taste with salt. Pour over the salsa, cover with plastic wrap, and chill in the refrigerator until required.

❺ Thread the seafood on to 8 skewers. Cook under the hot broiler, turning frequently, for 6–8 minutes, or until cooked and tender. Season and serve with the salsa.

# Seafood Phyllo Pockets

These decorative, crisp phyllo pastry pockets are filled with succulent salmon and tasty crabmeat.

## *makes 24*

3½ oz/100g canned red salmon, drained

3½ oz/100g canned crabmeat, drained

2 tbsp chopped fresh parsley

8 scallions, finely chopped

corn oil, for oiling

8 sheets phyllo pastry (about 8 x 12 inches/20 x 30 cm), thawed if frozen

melted butter, for brushing

## Method

❶ Preheat the oven to 400°F/200°C. Remove and discard the skin and bones from the salmon, place in a bowl, and flake the flesh with a fork. Remove and discard any cartilage from the crabmeat, place in another bowl, and flake with a fork. Divide the parsley and scallions between the bowls and mix well.

❷ Lightly oil a cookie sheet. Keep the phyllo pastry sheets covered with plastic wrap to prevent them drying out. Take a sheet of phyllo, brush with melted butter, then place a second sheet on top. Cut into 4-inch/10-cm squares. Place a teaspoonful of the salmon mixture on each square. Brush the edges of the pastry with melted butter, then draw together to make little pouches. Press to seal. Repeat with 2 more sheets of phyllo and the salmon mixture, then repeat with the remaining sheets of phyllo and the crabmeat mixture.

❸ Place the parcels on the cookie sheet and bake in the preheated oven for 15 minutes, until golden. Serve warm.

# Devils & Angels On Horseback

**Tempting morsels to bring out the devil in you and raise the party spirit, these are delicious, classic snacks on a stick.**

*makes 32*

| Devils | Angels |
|---|---|
| 8 rindless lean bacon strips | 8 rindless lean bacon strips |
| 8 canned anchovy fillets, drained | 16 smoked oysters, drained if canned |
| 16 blanched almonds | |
| 16 no-soak pitted prunes | |

## Method

❶ Preheat the oven to 400°F/200°C. For the Devils, cut each bacon strip lengthwise in half and gently stretch with the back of a knife. Cut each anchovy fillet lengthwise in half. Wrap an anchovy half around each almond and press them into the cavity where the pits have been removed from the prunes. Wrap a strip of bacon around each prune and secure with a wooden toothpick.

❷ For the Angels, cut each bacon strip lengthwise in half and gently stretch with the back of a knife. Wrap a bacon strip around each oyster and secure with a wooden toothpick.

❸ Place the Devils and Angels on a cookie sheet and cook in the preheated oven for 10–15 minutes, or until sizzling hot and the bacon is cooked. Serve hot.

# San Francisco Wings

**Chicken wings cooked in a wonderfully sticky, slightly spicy sauce never fail to please. They are delicious served hot or warm.**

## *makes 12*

5 tbsp dark soy sauce

2 tbsp dry sherry

1 tbsp rice vinegar

2-inch/5-cm strip of orange rind, pith removed

juice of 1 orange

1 tbsp raw brown sugar

1 star anise

1 tsp cornstarch, mixed to a paste with 3 tbsp water

1 tbsp finely chopped fresh gingerroot

1 tsp chili sauce

3 lb 5 oz/1.5 kg chicken wings

## Method

**❶** Preheat the oven to 400°F/200°C. Place the soy sauce, sherry, vinegar, orange rind, orange juice, sugar, and star anise in a pan and mix well. Bring to a boil over medium heat, then stir in the cornstarch paste. Continue to boil, stirring constantly, for 1 minute, or until thickened. Remove the pan from the heat and stir in the ginger and chili sauce.

**❷** Remove and discard the tips from the chicken wings and place the wings in a single layer in an ovenproof dish or roasting pan. Pour the sauce over the wings, turning and stirring to coat.

**❸** Bake in the preheated oven for 35–40 minutes, turning and basting with the sauce occasionally, until the chicken is tender and browned and the juices run clear when a skewer is inserted into the thickest part of the meat. Serve either hot or warm.

# Spareribs

**Terrific to eat but astonishingly messy, so provide plenty of paper napkins. Sticky ribs are easy to prepare and won't keep you away from your guests for long.**

*makes 30*

2 tbsp peanut or corn oil

1 onion, chopped

1 garlic clove, finely chopped

1 fresh green chile, seeded and

finely chopped

3 tbsp clear honey

2 tbsp tomato paste

1 tbsp white wine vinegar

pinch of chili powder

²/₃ cup chicken stock

1 lb 12 oz/800 g pork spareribs

## Method

❶ Preheat the oven to 375°F/190°C. Heat the oil in a heavy-bottom pan over medium heat. Add the onion, garlic, and chile and cook, stirring occasionally, for 5 minutes until softened. Stir in the honey, tomato paste, white wine vinegar, chili powder, and chicken stock and bring to a boil. Reduce the heat and simmer, stirring occasionally, for 15 minutes until thickened.

❷ Meanwhile, chop the spareribs into 2-inch/5-cm lengths and place in a roasting pan. Pour the sauce over them, turning and stirring to coat. Roast in the preheated oven for 1 hour, turning and basting with the sauce frequently, until the ribs are thoroughly browned and sticky.

❸ Remove from the oven and transfer to a warmed serving dish. Serve immediately.

# Indonesian Peanut Fritters

These crisp bites are so effortless that you can cook them when the party is in full swing. Equally, you can prepare them in advance and quickly reheat in the oven when required.

## *makes 20*

¼ cup rice flour

½ tsp baking powder

½ tsp ground turmeric

½ tsp ground coriander

¼ tsp ground cumin

1 garlic clove, finely chopped

½ cup unsalted peanuts, crushed

½–⅔ cup coconut milk

salt

peanut oil, for frying

## Method

❶ Combine the rice flour, baking powder, turmeric, coriander, cumin, garlic, and peanuts in a bowl. Gradually stir in enough coconut milk to make a smooth, thin batter. Season to taste with salt.

❷ Pour the oil into a heavy-bottom skillet to a depth of about ½ inch/1 cm and heat over high heat until hot. Add tablespoonfuls of the batter to the pan, spacing them well apart, and fry until the tops have just set and the undersides are golden. Turn the fritters over and cook for 1 minute until the second side is golden. Remove with a fish slice, drain on paper towels, and keep warm while you cook the remaining fritters. Serve immediately.

❸ Alternatively, transfer the fritters to wire racks to cool, then store in an airtight container. When ready to serve, preheat the oven to 350°F/180°C. Place the fritters on cookie sheets and reheat in the preheated oven for 10 minutes.

# Mini Pepperoni Pizzas

**Pizzas are always a firm favorite with party guests, and the biscuit base used here is much quicker and easier to make than a traditional bread dough base.**

*makes 12*

| Bases | Pepperoni topping |
|---|---|
| 4 cups self-rising flour, plus extra for dusting | ¾ cup ready-made tomato pizza sauce |
| 1 tsp salt | 4 oz/115 g rindless bacon, diced |
| 3 oz/85 g butter, diced | 1 orange bell pepper, seeded and chopped |
| 1¼–1½ cups milk | 3 oz/85 g pepperoni sausage, sliced |
| olive oil, for oiling | ½ cup grated mozzarella cheese |
| | ½ tsp dried oregano |
| | olive oil, for drizzling |
| | salt and pepper |

## Method

❶ Preheat the oven to 400°F/200°C. To make the bases, sift the flour and salt into a bowl, add the butter, and rub it in with your fingertips until the mixture resembles bread crumbs. Make a well in the center of the mixture and add 1¼ cups of the milk. Mix with the blade of a knife to a soft dough, adding the remaining milk if necessary.

❷ Turn out on to a lightly floured counter and knead gently. Divide the dough into 12 equal pieces and roll out each piece into a round. Place on a lightly oiled cookie sheet and gently push up the edges of each pizza to form a rim.

❸ For the topping, spread the tomato sauce over the bases almost to the edge. Arrange the bacon, bell pepper, and pepperoni on top and sprinkle with the cheese. Sprinkle with the oregano, drizzle with a little oil, and season to taste with salt and pepper.

❹ Bake in the preheated oven for 10–15 minutes, or until the edges are crisp and the cheese is bubbling. Serve.

# Mini Artichoke Pizzas

This recipe offers an alternative, equally tempting topping for the simple biscuit base featured on page 90. Make a mixed batch for a colorful addition to your party buffet.

## *makes 12*

### Bases

4 cups self-rising flour, plus extra
for dusting

1 tsp salt

3 oz/85 g butter, diced

1 1/4–1 1/2 cups milk

olive oil, for oiling

### Artichoke topping

3/4 cup ready-made tomato
pizza sauce

2 oz/55 g Gorgonzola cheese, sliced

4 oz/115 g canned artichoke hearts in oil,
drained and sliced

2 shallots, chopped

1/2 cup grated Gruyère cheese

4 tbsp freshly grated Parmesan cheese

1/2 tsp dried oregano

olive oil, for drizzling

salt and pepper

## Method

❶ Preheat the oven to 400°F/200°C. To prepare the bases, follow Steps 1 and 2 on page 90.

❷ For the topping, spread the tomato sauce over the bases almost to the edge. Arrange the Gorgonzola slices, artichoke hearts, and shallots on top. Mix together the Gruyère and Parmesan in a bowl and sprinkle over the pizzas. Sprinkle with the oregano, drizzle with oil, and season to taste with salt and pepper.

❸ Bake in the preheated oven for 10–15 minutes, or until the edges are crisp and the cheese is bubbling. Serve.

# Bruschetta

**These savory Italian toasts taste terrific and can be prepared in advance, ready to pop in the oven when your guests arrive.**

*makes 30*

3 thin ciabatta loaves or baguettes

½ cup green pesto

½ cup red pesto

1 lb/450 g mozzarella cheese, diced

2 tsp dried oregano

pepper

3 tbsp olive oil

## Method

❶ Preheat the oven to 425°F/220°C and the broiler to medium. Slice the loaves diagonally and discard the crusty ends. Toast the slices on both sides under the hot broiler until golden.

❷ Spread one side of each slice of toast with either green or red pesto and top with the mozzarella. Sprinkle with the oregano and season to taste with pepper.

❸ Place the bruschetta on a large cookie sheet and drizzle with the oil. Bake in the preheated oven for 5 minutes, or until the cheese has melted and is bubbling. Remove the bruschetta from the oven and let stand for 5 minutes before serving.

# Pigs in Blankets

This is a more interesting version of the ever-popular sausages on sticks. For extra variety, use a mixture of differently flavored sausages.

## makes 48

16 large, good-quality sausages

4 tbsp Dijon mustard

48 no-soak pitted prunes

16 rindless bacon strips

## Method

❶ Preheat the broiler to medium. Cut a deep slit along the length of each sausage without cutting all the way through. Spread the mustard evenly over the cut sides of the slits. Place 3 prunes inside each slit, pressing the sausages together.

❷ Gently stretch each bacon strip with the back of a knife. Wind a strip around each sausage to hold it together.

❸ Cook under the hot broiler, turning frequently, for 15 minutes, or until cooked through. Transfer to a cutting board and cut each "pig" into 3 pieces, each containing a prune. Spear with wooden toothpicks, arrange on a plate, and serve.

# Barbecue Food

Cooking food outdoors on a grill is great fun and a delicious way of feeding a crowd. To keep everybody happy, it is always a good idea to offer a range of meat and seafood dishes, vegetables, salads, and desserts, so that there is something for meat-eaters, vegetarians, and even fussy children.

The dishes can be as straightforward or complicated as you wish. You can start by elaborate dishes. Thread seafood, poultry, vegetables, or fruits on to wooden skewers to make kabobs. Add extra flavor and succulence to the food by mixing various marinades and dressings.

The key to a successful barbecue is good planning. It helps to know roughly how many people are coming. If the numbers are very vague or large, you need to lay on a plentiful supply of

basics, such as burgers, salad, and bread, so that nobody goes hungry. Reserve supplies can be kept in the refrigerator and frozen later if not needed.

cooking a basic barbecue with traditional ingredients such as burgers, chicken drumsticks, chops, steaks, and sausages. Served with burger buns, French bread or baked potatoes, and plenty of fresh leafy or mixed salad, good food doesn't get much easier.

Once you have got the hang of cooking on your grill, you can experiment with more

To cater for vegetarian guests, prepare plenty of vegetable kabobs and pockets which others can eat, too. Offer different fillings to go with baked potatoes: a creamy cheese or a spicy corn relish are very popular. A good selection of colorful salads, including a pasta, rice, tomato, or mixed bean salad, will please vegetarians and appeal to everyone else as well.

Before you start a barbecue party, you should consider the safety aspects—grilling is a safe way of cooking as long as you take a few sensible precautions.

• Position your grill away from overhanging trees and shrubs to avoid branches catching fire. Have a bucket of water nearby in case the fire blows out of control.

• Trim off excess fat and shake away surplus marinade before putting the food on the grill to stop fat dripping down on to the hot coals and bursting into flames.

• To minimize the risk of food poisoning, make sure that meat and seafood are cooked through. Test the meat by piercing it with a skewer or the tip of a sharp knife—it is cooked when the juices run clear (not pink). Once poultry has cooled down, never return it to the grill to finish cooking.

• Keep salads and cooked foods away from raw meat. Use different cutting boards, utensils, dish towels, and plates for dealing with raw and cooked meats or salad ingredients.

• On hot days, store foods out of direct sunlight and keep them chilled for as long as possible before cooking or serving. Cover food with netting or clean dish towels to keep insects off.

• Never leave the grill unattended. Warn any small children to keep away from the hot fire. Ban pets from the food and cooking areas as well, to prevent contamination and accidents.

• Use long-handled utensils and oven mitts to avoid getting burned and splashed.

• Anyone who will be involved in the cooking should go easy on the alcohol.

## Types of Fuel

There are many different types of fuel on the market so you should consider your exact requirements before you spend any money.

• Lumpwood charcoal is readily available, inexpensive, and easy to light, but burns quickly.

• Charcoal briquettes take longer to catch, but burn for a long time and produce little smoke.

• Self-igniting charcoal is lumpwood charcoal or charcoal briquettes that have been coated with a flammable chemical. They light easily but you cannot start cooking until the chemical has burned off as it can taint the food.

• Wood fires need constant attention. Hardwoods, such as mesquite, oak, and apple, are best as they burn slowly and have a pleasant smell. Softwoods, however, burn too fast and tend to spark.

• Wood chips and herbs, such as sprigs of thyme or rosemary, can be sprinkled on the fire to give off a delicious aroma.

## Choosing Your Grill

Before buying a grill, consider the number of people you will want to feed; how often you are likely to use it; how it will fit into your backyard; if you need one that is portable; and how much you are prepared to spend on it.

• Disposable grills are inexpensive foil trays with enough fuel to burn for about an hour—ideal for a small, one-off picnic.

• Hibachi or "firebox" grills from Japan are small, lightweight, reusable, and easy to transport.

• Portable grills are light and easy to fold up and carry in the trunk of a car for larger picnics.

• Brazier grills can be moved about the backyard and stored easily. Some are a little low, so check that the one you are thinking of buying is a comfortable height for the person who will be doing most of the cooking. If your yard gets windy, choose a grill with a hood to protect the open grill.

• Kettle-grills are the next best thing to a permanent grill. The lid covers the grill and can save a barbecue party if it starts to rain. Many kettle-grills have a rotisserie for cooking chickens and joints.

• Gas and electric grills are expensive but easy to operate and very quick—they only take ten minutes to warm up. However, they do not give the food the traditional smoky flavor it gets from being cooked over charcoal.

• Permanent, tailor-made grills are an excellent choice if you grill frequently. You can buy kits or use simple materials such as house- and fire-bricks to build a fireplace and fit an adjustable metal rack.

## Preparation

It is possible to make some dishes for your grill, such as burgers and kabobs, well in advance and freeze them—all you have to do is take them out the night before and thaw them thoroughly. Alternatively, you can make them the previous day and store them in the refrigerator overnight. You may also start marinating food the day before.

Leave the chopping and mixing of any salad ingredients until the morning of the barbecue. Toss in the dressing just before you are ready to serve them, so that the leaves and other ingredients do not go limp and soggy.

## Hints & Tips

• Remember to light your grill at least an hour before you want to start cooking to make sure it will be hot. For setting the fire, follow the instructions that come with the fuel you are using.

• To ensure even and thorough cooking, do not place too much food on the grill rack at once.

• Aim to cook the same types of food together to avoid contamination. Do not mix meat, fish, and vegetarian dishes on the grill. The best plan is to wrap the vegetarian ingredients in foil pockets.

• Foil-wrapped potatoes cook well, especially if you bake them in a conventional oven at 400°F/200°C for 30 minutes before moving them to the grill to finish cooking.

• Foil pockets are often the best solution for hot desserts. Just wrap the fruits and let cook around the edge of the grill where the temperature is slightly lower.

• Offer a choice of drinks, both alcoholic and non-alcoholic: a fruit punch is usually popular.

• Even when rained out, you can keep cooking if you shut the lid of your grill and open the vents. Alternatively, you can take the food inside and carry on cooking under the broiler in your kitchen. When the sun appears again, you can move back outside.

Meat & Poultry

# Tabasco Steaks with Parsley Butter

**A variation on a classic theme, this simple but rather extravagant dish is ideal for a special-occasion barbecue party.**

*serves 4*

1 bunch of parsley

6 tbsp unsalted butter, softened

4 sirloin steaks, about 8 oz/225 g each

4 tsp Tabasco sauce

salt and pepper

## Method

❶ Preheat the grill. Using a sharp knife, finely chop enough parsley to fill 4 tablespoons. Reserve a few parsley leaves for the garnish. Place the butter in a small bowl and beat in the chopped parsley with a fork until fully incorporated. Cover with plastic wrap and let chill in the refrigerator until required.

❷ Sprinkle each steak with 1 teaspoon of the Tabasco sauce, rubbing it in well. Season to taste with salt and pepper.

❸ Cook the steaks over hot coals: 2½ minutes each side for rare, 4 minutes each side for medium, and 6 minutes each side for well done. Transfer to serving plates, garnish with the reserved parsley leaves, and serve immediately, topped with the parsley butter.

## Variation

*If you can find watercress, substitute for the same amount of fresh parsley, if you prefer.*

# Best Ever Burgers

Barbecues and burgers are almost inseparable. However, these succulent, homemade burgers bear no resemblance to the little ready-made patties available in most stores.

*serves 6*

2 lb/900 g lean ground chuck

2 onions, finely chopped

½ cup fresh white bread crumbs

1 egg, lightly beaten

1½ teaspoons finely chopped fresh thyme

salt and pepper

To serve

6 sesame seed hamburger buns

2 tomatoes

1 onion

lettuce leaves

mayonnaise

mustard

tomato ketchup

## Method

❶ Preheat the grill. Place the meat, onions, bread crumbs, egg, and thyme in a large glass bowl and season to taste with salt and pepper. Mix thoroughly using your hands.

❷ Form the mixture into 6 large burgers with your hands, neatening the edges with a round-bladed knife.

❸ Cook the burgers over hot coals for 3-4 minutes on each side. Meanwhile, cut the buns in half and briefly toast on the grill, cut-side down. Using a sharp knife, slice the tomatoes and cut the onion into thinly sliced rings. Fill the toasted buns with the cooked burgers, lettuce, tomato slices, and onion rings and serve immediately with the mayonnaise, mustard, and tomato ketchup.

## Variation

*For Tex-Mex burgers, add 2 seeded and finely chopped fresh green chiles to the mixture in Step 1 and serve with Guacamole (see page 20).*

# Luxury Cheeseburgers

This is a sophisticated version of the traditional burger with a surprise filling of melted blue cheese. Serve with plenty of salad to make a substantial barbecue lunch.

## serves 4

2 oz/55 g Stilton cheese

1 lb/450 g lean ground chuck

1 onion, finely chopped

1 celery stalk, finely chopped

1 tsp creamed horseradish

1 tbsp chopped fresh thyme

salt and pepper

To serve

4 sesame seed hamburger buns

lettuce leaves

sliced tomatoes

## Method

❶ Preheat the grill. Crumble the Stilton cheese into a bowl and reserve until required. Place the steak, onion, celery, horseradish, and thyme in a separate bowl and season to taste with salt and pepper. Mix thoroughly using your hands.

❷ Form the mixture into 8 burgers with your hands and a round-bladed knife. Divide the cheese between 4 of them and top with the remaining burgers. Gently press them together and mold the edges.

❸ Cook the burgers over hot coals for 5 minutes on each side. Meanwhile, cut the buns in half and briefly toast on the grill, cut side down. Fill the buns with the cooked burgers, lettuce, and tomato slices and serve immediately.

## Variation

*Substitute Saga blue, Cheddar, or Swiss cheese for the Stilton cheese and finely snipped chives for the thyme.*

# Rack & Ruin

**This quick and easy dish is perfect for serving as part of a summer party menu, along with plenty of salad and potatoes.**

*serves 4*

4 racks of lamb, each with 4 rib chops

2 tbsp extra virgin olive oil

1 tbsp balsamic vinegar

1 tbsp lemon juice

3 tbsp finely chopped fresh rosemary

1 small onion, finely chopped

salt and pepper

## Method

❶ Place the racks of lamb in a large, shallow, nonmetallic dish. Make a marinade by placing the oil, vinegar, lemon juice, rosemary, and onion in a pitcher and stirring together. Season to taste with salt and pepper.

❷ Pour the marinade over the lamb and turn until thoroughly coated. Cover with plastic wrap and let marinate in the refrigerator for 1 hour, turning occasionally.

❸ Preheat the grill. Drain the racks of lamb, reserving the marinade. Cook over medium-hot coals, brushing frequently with the marinade, for 10 minutes on each side. Serve immediately.

# Minted Lamb Steaks

You can prepare this dish with any kind of lamb chops—leg chops are especially tender—or rib chops, in which case you will probably require two per serving. Shoulder steaks also work well.

### serves 6

6 lamb chops, about 6 oz/175 g each

²/₃ cup strained plain yogurt

2 garlic cloves, finely chopped

1 tsp grated fresh gingerroot

¼ tsp coriander seeds, crushed

salt and pepper

1 tbsp olive oil, plus extra for brushing

1 tbsp orange juice

1 tsp walnut oil

2 tbsp chopped fresh mint

## Method

❶ Place the chops in a large, shallow, nonmetallic bowl. Mix half the yogurt, the garlic, ginger, and coriander seeds together in a pitcher and season to taste with salt and pepper. Spoon the mixture over the chops, turning to coat them evenly, then cover with plastic wrap and let marinate in the refrigerator for 2 hours, turning occasionally.

❷ Preheat the grill. Place the remaining yogurt, the olive oil, orange juice, walnut oil, and mint in a small bowl and, using a hand-held whisk, whisk until thoroughly blended. Season to taste with salt and pepper. Cover the minted yogurt with plastic wrap and let chill in the refrigerator until ready to serve.

❸ Drain the chops, scraping off the marinade. Brush with olive oil and cook over medium-hot coals for 5–7 minutes on each side. Serve immediately with the minted yogurt.

## Variation

*If you like, omit the orange juice and walnut oil and stir in ¼ teaspoon ground star anise and a pinch each of ground cinnamon and ground cumin.*

# Normandy Brochettes

The orchards of Normandy are famous throughout France, providing both eating apples and hard cider-making varieties. For an authentic touch, enjoy a glass of Calvados between courses.

*serves 4*

1 lb/450 g pork tenderloin

1¼ cups hard cider

1 tbsp finely chopped fresh sage

6 black peppercorns, crushed

2 crisp eating apples

1 tbsp corn oil

## Method

❶ Using a sharp knife, cut the pork into 1-inch/2.5-cm cubes, then place in a large, shallow, nonmetallic dish. Mix the hard cider, sage, and peppercorns together in a pitcher, pour the mixture over the pork, and turn until thoroughly coated. Cover with plastic wrap and let marinate in the refrigerator for 1–2 hours.

❷ Preheat the grill. Drain the pork, reserving the marinade. Core the apples, but do not peel them, then cut into wedges. Dip the apple wedges into the reserved marinade and thread on to several flat metal skewers, alternating with the cubes of pork. Stir the oil into the remaining marinade.

❸ Cook the brochettes over medium-hot coals, turning and brushing frequently with the marinade, for 12–15 minutes. Transfer to a large serving plate and, if you prefer, remove the meat and apples from the skewers before serving. Serve immediately.

## Variation

*Replace 1 apple with 6 no-soak pitted prunes wrapped in strips of bacon. Thread the prunes on to the skewers with the remaining apple and pork.*

# Sausages with Barbecue Sauce

**Although there is much more to barbecues than sausages, they can make a welcome appearance from time to time. This delicious sauce is a wonderful excuse for including them again.**

*serves 4*

2 tbsp corn oil

1 large onion, chopped

2 garlic cloves, chopped

1 cup canned chopped tomatoes

1 tbsp Worcestershire sauce

2 tbsp fruity brown sauce

2 tbsp raw brown sugar

4 tbsp white wine vinegar

½ tsp mild chili powder

¼ tsp mustard powder

dash of Tabasco sauce

salt and pepper

1 lb/450 g sausages

finger bread rolls, to serve

## Method

❶ Preheat the grill. To make the sauce, heat the oil in a small pan and fry the onion and garlic for 4–5 minutes, or until softened and just beginning to brown.

❷ Add the tomatoes, Worcestershire sauce, brown sauce, sugar, vinegar, chili powder, mustard powder, and Tabasco sauce to the pan. Add salt and pepper to taste, and bring to a boil.

❸ Reduce the heat and simmer gently for 10–15 minutes, or until the sauce begins to thicken slightly. Stir occasionally so that the sauce does not burn and stick to the bottom of the pan. Set aside and keep warm until required.

❹ Cook the sausages over hot coals for 10–15 minutes, turning frequently. Do not prick them with a fork or the juices and fat will run out and cause the grill to flare.

❺ Insert the sausages into the bread rolls and serve with the barbecue sauce.

## Variation

*Choose any tasty "country" sausages for this recipe. Also try chorizo, frankfurter, Italian, and Toulouse sausages.*

# Meatballs on Sticks

These are popular with children and adults alike. Serve with a selection
of ready-made or homemade sauces, such as a tomato relish, heated on
the side of the grill, or Spicy Salsa (see page 78).

## *serves 8*

4 pork and herb sausages

4 oz/115 g ground beef

1½ cups fresh white bread crumbs

1 onion, finely chopped

2 tbsp chopped mixed fresh herbs,
such as parsley, thyme, and sage

1 egg

salt and pepper

corn oil, for brushing

sauces of choice, to serve

## Method

❶ Preheat the grill. Remove the sausage meat from the skins, place in a large bowl, and break up with a fork. Add the ground beef, bread crumbs, onion, herbs, and egg. Season to taste with salt and pepper and stir well with a wooden spoon until thoroughly mixed.

❷ Form the mixture into small balls, about the size of a golf ball, between the palms of your hands. Spear each one with a wooden toothpick and brush with oil.

❸ Cook over medium-hot coals, turning frequently and brushing with more oil as necessary, for 10 minutes, or until cooked through. Transfer to a large serving plate and serve immediately with a choice of sauces.

## Variation

*Substitute 1 cooked potato and 1 cooked small beet, both finely chopped, for the bread crumbs.*

# Bacon Koftas

Koftas—molded kabobs—are usually made from a spicy mixture of ground lamb. These ones are economically based on lean bacon. While they are very easy to make, be careful not to over-process them.

*serves 4*

1 small onion

8 oz/225 g lean bacon, rinded and coarsely chopped

1½ cups fresh white bread crumbs

1 tbsp chopped fresh marjoram

grated rind of 1 lemon

1 egg white

pepper

paprika, for dusting

chopped nuts, for coating (optional)

fresh chives lengths, to garnish

bulgur wheat or couscous salad, to serve

## Method

❶ Preheat the grill. Using a sharp knife, chop the onion, then place it in a food processor with the bacon, bread crumbs, marjoram, lemon rind, and egg white. Season to taste with pepper and process briefly, just until the mixture is blended.

❷ Divide the bacon mixture into 8 equal portions and form each around a skewer into a fat sausage. Dust the skewered koftas with paprika. If you like, form 4 of the portions into rounds rather than sausages, then spread the chopped nuts out on a large, flat plate and roll the rounds in them to coat.

❸ Cook over hot coals for 10 minutes, turning frequently. Transfer to a large serving plate and serve immediately, garnished with fresh chives lengths.

# Fabulous Frankfurter Skewers

**A new way with an old favorite—cook frankfurters on the grill for a wonderful smoky flavor and an incredibly easy meal. They are served here with Garlic Toast.**

*serves 4*

| | |
|---|---|
| 12 frankfurters | Garlic toast |
| 2 zucchini, cut into ½-inch/1-cm slices | 2 garlic bulbs |
| 2 corn cobs, cut into ½-inch/1-cm slices | 2–3 tbsp olive oil |
| 12 cherry tomatoes | 1 baguette, sliced |
| 12 pearl onions | salt and pepper |
| 2 tbsp olive oil | |

## Method

❶ Preheat the grill. To make the Garlic Toast, slice off the tops of the garlic bulbs. Brush the bulbs with oil and wrap them in foil. Cook over hot coals, turning occasionally, for 30 minutes.

❷ Meanwhile, cut each of the frankfurters into 3 pieces. Thread the frankfurter pieces, zucchini slices, corn cob slices, tomatoes, and onions alternately on to flat metal skewers. Brush with oil.

❸ Cook the skewers over hot coals, turning and brushing frequently with the oil, for 8–10 minutes. Meanwhile, brush the slices of baguette with the remaining oil and toast both sides on the grill. Unwrap the garlic bulbs and squeeze the cloves on to the bread. Season to taste with salt and pepper and drizzle over a little extra oil, if desired. Transfer the skewers to a large serving plate and serve immediately with the Garlic Toast.

## Variation

*Serve with Garlic Bread in place of Garlic Toast. Slice a baguette without cutting it right through. Spread with 2 crushed garlic cloves beaten into ½ cup butter. Wrap in foil and cook for 15 minutes.*

# Chicken Tikka

This colorful dish looks immensely appetizing and the aroma as it cooks is out of this world—it lives up to its promise, too.

## serves 4

1 lb 2 oz/500 g skinless, boneless chicken, cut into 2-inch/5-cm cubes

1 garlic clove, finely chopped

½-inch/1-cm piece fresh gingerroot, finely chopped

⅔ cup plain yogurt

4 tbsp lemon juice

1 tsp chili powder

¼ tsp ground turmeric

1 tbsp chopped fresh cilantro

vegetable oil, for brushing

naan bread, to serve

Raita

½ cucumber

1 fresh green chile, seeded and finely chopped

1¼ cups plain yogurt

¼ tsp ground cumin

salt

To garnish

thinly sliced onion rings

fresh cilantro sprigs

lemon wedges

# Method

❶ Place the chicken in a large, nonmetallic bowl. Add the garlic, gingerroot, yogurt, lemon juice, chili powder, turmeric, and cilantro and stir well. Cover with plastic wrap and let marinate in the refrigerator for up to 8 hours.

❷ Preheat the grill. To make the raita, cut the cucumber into thick slices, then finely chop. Place the cucumber and chile in a bowl and beat in the yogurt with a fork. Stir in the cumin and season to taste with salt. Cover and let chill in the refrigerator until required.

❸ Thread the chicken cubes on to presoaked wooden skewers and brush with oil. Cook the chicken over medium-hot coals, turning and brushing frequently with oil, for 15 minutes, or until thoroughly cooked. Briefly heat the naan bread on the grill. Remove the chicken from the skewers and place on individual serving plates. Garnish with onion rings, cilantro sprigs, and lemon wedges, and serve with the naan bread and the raita.

# Sage & Lemon Squab Chickens

**Spatchcocked squab chickens are the ideal choice for a barbecue, as they are easy to handle and look attractive.**

## *serves 4*

| | |
|---|---|
| 4 squab chickens, about 1 lb/450 g each | To garnish |
| 1 lemon | fresh herb sprigs, such as sage |
| 2 tbsp chopped fresh sage | lemon slices |
| salt and pepper | |

## Method

❶ Preheat the grill. To spatchcock the squab chickens, turn one bird breast-side down and, using strong kitchen scissors or poultry shears, cut through the skin and ribcage along both sides of the backbone, from tail to neck. Remove the backbone and turn the bird breast-side up. Flatten the breastbone with the heel of your hand. Fold the wingtips underneath. Repeat with the remaining birds.

❷ Thinly slice half the lemon and finely grate the rind of the other half. Mix the lemon rind and sage together in a small bowl. Loosen the skin over the breasts and legs of the squab chickens and insert the lemon and sage mixture. Tuck in the lemon slices and smooth the skin back firmly. Push a flat metal skewer into one wing, through the top of the breast, and out of the other wing. Push a second skewer into one thigh, through the bottom of the breast, and out of the other thigh. Season to taste with salt and pepper.

❸ Cook the squab chickens over medium-hot coals for 10–15 minutes on each side, or until thoroughly cooked. Serve immediately, garnished with herb sprigs and lemon slices.

# Hot Red Chicken

Chicken pieces are used in this adaptation of a traditional Indian recipe for spring chickens, but you could substitute spatchcocked squab chickens if you prefer (see page 128).

*serves 4*

1 tbsp curry paste

1 tbsp tomato ketchup

1 tsp five-spice powder

1 fresh red chile, seeded and finely chopped

1 tsp Worcestershire sauce

1 tsp sugar

salt

8 skinless chicken pieces

vegetable oil, for brushing

**To garnish**

lemon wedges

fresh cilantro sprigs

naan bread, to serve

## Method

❶ Place the curry paste, tomato ketchup, five-spice powder, chile, Worcestershire sauce, and sugar in a small bowl and stir until the sugar has dissolved. Season to taste with salt.

❷ Place the chicken pieces in a large, shallow, nonmetallic dish and spoon the spice paste over them, rubbing in well. Cover with plastic wrap and let marinate in the refrigerator for up to 8 hours.

❸ Preheat the grill. Remove the chicken from the spice paste, discarding any remaining paste, and brush with oil. Cook the chicken over medium-hot coals, turning occasionally, for 25–30 minutes, or until tender and the juices run clear when a skewer is inserted into the thickest part of the meat. Briefly heat the naan bread on the grill and serve with the chicken, garnished with lemon wedges and cilantro sprigs.

# Turkey Rolls

These herb-flavored rolls conceal a soft center of melted cheese as a lovely surprise. They are served here with red currant relish, but are also delicious with a mild mustard sauce.

*serves 4*

| | |
|---|---|
| 2 tbsp corn oil | **Red currant relish** |
| salt and pepper | 1 cup red currants |
| 4 tbsp chopped fresh marjoram | 2 tbsp chopped fresh mint |
| 4 turkey breast steaks | 2 tsp clear honey |
| 4 tsp mild mustard | 1 tsp red wine vinegar |
| 6 oz/175 g Emmental cheese, grated | salt and pepper |
| 1 leek, thinly sliced | |

# Method

❶ Preheat the grill. To make the red currant relish, place all the ingredients in a bowl and mash well with a fork. Season to taste with salt and pepper. Cover with plastic wrap and let chill in the refrigerator until required.

❷ Pour the oil into a small bowl, season to taste with pepper, and stir in 2 teaspoons of the marjoram. Reserve. Place the turkey steaks between 2 sheets of plastic wrap and beat with the side of a rolling pin to flatten. Season to taste with salt and pepper and spread the mustard evenly over them. Divide the cheese, leek, and remaining marjoram between the turkey steaks, roll up, and tie securely with kitchen string.

❸ Brush the turkey rolls with the flavored oil and cook over medium-hot coals, turning and brushing frequently with the remaining oil, for 30 minutes. Serve immediately with the relish.

# Variation

*The red currant relish can be replaced with cranberry relish if preferred.*

# Tarragon Turkey

**This economical dish is quick and simple to prepare, and yet tastes absolutely wonderful, not least because poultry and tarragon have a natural affinity.**

*serves 4*

4 turkey breast steaks, about 6 oz/175 g each

salt and pepper

4 tsp whole-grain mustard

8 fresh tarragon sprigs, plus extra to garnish

4 Canadian bacon strips

salad greens, to serve

## Method

❶ Preheat the grill. Season the turkey to taste with salt and pepper and, using a round-bladed knife, spread the mustard evenly over the turkey.

❷ Place 2 tarragon sprigs on top of each turkey breast and wrap a bacon strip around to hold the herbs in place. Secure with a wooden toothpick.

❸ Cook the turkey over medium-hot coals for 5–8 minutes on each side. Transfer to serving plates and garnish with tarragon sprigs. Serve with salad greens.

# Fruity Duck

Apricots and onions counteract the richness of the duck. Its high fat content makes it virtually self-basting, so it stays superbly moist. The duck looks particularly elegant garnished with scallion tassels.

*serves 4*

4 duck breasts

⅔ cup no-soak dried apricots

2 shallots, thinly sliced

2 tbsp clear honey

1 tsp sesame oil

2 tsp Chinese five-spice powder

4 scallions, to garnish

## Method

❶ Preheat the grill. Using a sharp knife, cut a long slit in the fleshy side of each duck breast to make a pocket. Divide the apricots and shallots between the pockets and secure with skewers.

❷ Mix the honey and oil together in a small bowl and brush all over the duck. Sprinkle with the five-spice powder. To make the garnish, make a few cuts lengthwise down the stem of each scallion. Place in a bowl of ice water and let stand until the tassels open out. Drain well before using.

❸ Cook the duck over medium-hot coals for 6–8 minutes on each side. Remove the skewers, transfer to a large serving plate, and garnish with the scallion tassels. Serve immediately.

## Variation

*Substitute 4 pork chops for the duck and cook over medium-hot coals for 8–9 minutes on each side, or until thoroughly cooked.*

Fish
& Seafood

# Caribbean Fish Kabobs

**Lightly spiced and marinated, these colorful kabobs look and taste delicious. You can use any firm-textured fish, but for an authentic Caribbean flavor, swordfish is perfect.**

## serves 6

2 lb 4 oz/1 kg swordfish steaks

3 tbsp olive oil

3 tbsp lime juice

1 garlic clove, finely chopped

1 tsp paprika

salt and pepper

3 onions, cut into wedges

6 tomatoes, cut into wedges

## Method

❶ Using a sharp knife, cut the fish into 1-inch/2.5-cm cubes and place in a shallow, nonmetallic dish. Place the oil, lime juice, garlic, and paprika in a pitcher and mix well. Season to taste with salt and pepper. Pour the marinade over the fish, turning to coat evenly. Cover with plastic wrap and let marinate in the refrigerator for 1 hour.

❷ Preheat the grill. Thread the fish cubes, onion wedges, and tomato wedges alternately on to 6 long, presoaked wooden skewers. Reserve the marinade.

❸ Cook the kabobs over medium-hot coals for 8–10 minutes, turning and brushing frequently with the reserved marinade. When they are cooked through, transfer the kabobs to a large serving plate and serve immediately.

## Variation

*Instead of serving the kabobs with traditional baked potatoes, serve them with baked sweet potatoes.*

# Salmon with Mango Salsa

**Although an oily fish, salmon can dry out easily on the fierce heat of the grill.
Make sure that it is well coated with the citrus juice before you begin cooking.**

### serves 4

4 salmon steaks, about 6 oz/175 g each

finely grated rind and juice of 1 lime or
½ lemon

salt and pepper

Salsa

1 large mango, peeled, pitted,
and diced

1 red onion, finely chopped

2 passion fruit

2 fresh basil sprigs

2 tbsp lime juice

## Method

❶ Preheat the grill. Rinse the salmon steaks under cold running water, pat dry with paper towels, and place in a large, shallow, nonmetallic dish. Sprinkle with the lime rind and pour the juice over them. Season to taste with salt and pepper, cover, and let stand while you make the salsa.

❷ Place the mango flesh in a bowl with the onion. Cut the passion fruit in half and scoop out the seeds and the pulp with a teaspoon. Add to the bowl. Tear the basil leaves and add them to the bowl with the lime juice. Season to taste with salt and stir well. Cover with plastic wrap and reserve until required.

❸ Cook the salmon steaks over medium-hot coals for 3–4 minutes on each side. Serve immediately with the salsa.

# Stuffed Sardines

**Grilled fresh sardines are always a popular choice. They are usually just plainly grilled, but here they are stuffed with herbs and coated in a mild spice mixture.**

## *serves 6*

| | |
|---|---|
| ¼ cup fresh parsley, finely chopped | ⅔ cup all-purpose flour |
| 4 garlic cloves, finely chopped | 1 tsp ground cumin |
| 12 fresh sardines, gutted and scaled | salt and pepper |
| 3 tbsp lemon juice | olive oil, for brushing |

# Method

**❶** Place the parsley and garlic in a bowl and mix together. Rinse the fish inside and out under cold running water and pat dry with paper towels. Spoon the herb mixture into the fish cavities and pat the remainder all over the outside of the fish. Sprinkle the sardines with lemon juice and transfer to a large, shallow, nonmetallic dish. Cover with plastic wrap and let marinate in the refrigerator for 1 hour.

**❷** Preheat the grill. Mix the flour and cumin together in a bowl, then season to taste with salt and pepper. Spread out the seasoned flour on a large plate and gently roll the sardines in the flour to coat.

**❸** Brush the sardines with oil and cook over medium-hot coals for 3–4 minutes on each side. Serve immediately.

# Orange & Lemon Peppered Angler Fish

Although angler fish appears quite expensive, there is very little wastage as, apart from the central backbone, the entire tail is edible. Its flavor is meaty and succulent.

## serves 6

2 oranges

2 lemons

2 angler fish tails, about 1 lb 2 oz/500 g each, skinned and cut into 4 fillets

6 fresh lemon thyme sprigs

2 tbsp olive oil

salt

2 tbsp green peppercorns, lightly crushed

**To garnish**

orange wedges

lemon wedges

## Method

❶ Cut 8 orange slices and 8 lemon slices, reserving the remaining fruit. Rinse the angler fish fillets under cold running water and pat dry with paper towels. Place 1 fillet from each fish tail, cut-side up, on a counter and divide the orange and lemon slices between them. Top with the lemon thyme. Reassemble the tails and tie them securely together at intervals with kitchen string or trussing thread. Place the tails in a large, shallow, nonmetallic dish.

❷ Squeeze the juice from the remaining fruit and mix with the oil in a pitcher. Season to taste with salt, then spoon the mixture over the fish. Cover with plastic wrap and let marinate in the refrigerator for up to 1 hour, spooning the marinade over the fish tails once or twice.

❸ Preheat the grill. Drain the fish tails, reserving the marinade. Sprinkle the crushed green peppercorns over the fish, pressing them in with your fingers. Cook the fish over medium-hot coals, turning and brushing frequently with the reserved marinade, for 20–25 minutes. Transfer to a cutting board, remove and discard the string, and cut the fish tails into slices. Serve immediately, garnished with orange and lemon wedges.

# Bacon-Wrapped Trout

This classic, pan-fried combination is even more delicious cooked on the grill,
as the smoky flavor of the bacon becomes more pronounced in contrast to
the delicate flesh of the fish.

*serves 4*

4 trout, cleaned and scaled

4 bacon strips

4 tbsp all-purpose flour

salt and pepper

2 tbsp olive oil

2 tbsp lemon juice

To garnish

fresh parsley sprigs

lemon wedges

mâche, to serve

## Method

❶ Preheat the grill. Rinse the trout inside and out under cold running water and pat dry with paper towels. Cut off any rind and stretch the bacon using the back of a heavy, flat-bladed knife.

❷ Season the flour to taste with salt and pepper and spread it out on a large, flat plate. Gently roll each trout in the seasoned flour until thoroughly coated. Beginning just below the head, wrap a bacon strip in a spiral along the length of each fish.

❸ Brush the trout with oil and cook over medium-hot coals for 5–8 minutes on each side, or until cooked through and the bacon is browned and crispy. Transfer to 4 large serving plates and drizzle with the lemon juice. Garnish with parsley sprigs and lemon wedges and serve with mâche.

# Sizzling Scallops

**This is a great new way to cook scallops on the grill. You can also use other shellfish, such as oysters, if you prefer.**

*serves 4*

rind of 1 lemon

6 tbsp olive oil

salt and pepper

12 prepared scallops

2 cups fresh whole-wheat bread crumbs

4 tbsp butter, melted

lemon wedges, to garnish (optional)

## Method

❶ Finely grate the lemon rind, then place it in a dish with the oil and mix together. Season to taste with salt and pepper. Add the scallops, tossing to coat, then cover and let marinate in the refrigerator for 30 minutes.

❷ Preheat the grill. Place the bread crumbs in a large bowl. Add the scallops, one at a time, and toss until they are well coated, then thread on to individual presoaked wooden skewers. Drizzle with the melted butter.

❸ Cook the breaded scallops over medium-hot coals, turning once, for 8–10 minutes, or until just cooked. Transfer to a large serving dish, garnish with lemon wedges, if desired, and serve immediately.

# Chargrilled Devils

This is a barbecue version of the classic appetizer "angels on horseback," and goes to prove how sophisticated and elegant alfresco dining can be.

*serves 4*

36 fresh oysters

18 bacon strips

1 tbsp mild paprika

1 tsp cayenne pepper

Sauce

1 fresh red chile, seeded and finely chopped

1 garlic clove, finely chopped

1 shallot, finely chopped

2 tbsp finely chopped fresh parsley

2 tbsp lemon juice

salt and pepper

## Method

❶ Preheat the grill. Open the oysters, catching the juice from the shells in a nonmetallic bowl. Cut the oysters from the bottom shells, reserve, and tip any remaining juice into the bowl. To make the sauce, add the chile, garlic, shallot, parsley, and lemon juice to the bowl, then season to taste with salt and pepper and mix well. Cover the bowl with plastic wrap and let chill in the refrigerator until required.

❷ Remove any rind and cut each bacon strip in half across the center. Season the oysters with paprika and cayenne, then roll each one up in half a bacon strip. Spear each wrapped oyster with a presoaked wooden toothpick or thread 9 on to each of 4 presoaked wooden skewers.

❸ Cook over hot coals, turning frequently, for 5 minutes, or until the bacon is well browned and crispy. Transfer to a large serving plate and serve immediately with the sauce.

## Variation

*You can replace the shallot with a small, finely chopped onion and the fresh parsley with the same amount of snipped fresh chives, if you prefer.*

# Spanish Shrimp

**These fresh shrimp are served with a fiery tomato and chili sauce. If you prefer a milder flavor, you can reduce the number of chiles.**

## *serves 6*

1 bunch of fresh flatleaf parsley

36 large, raw shrimp, shelled, tails left intact, and deveined

3–4 tbsp olive oil

lemon wedges, to garnish

### Sauce

6 fresh red chiles

1 onion, chopped

2 garlic cloves, chopped

1 lb/450 g tomatoes, chopped

3 tbsp olive oil

pinch of sugar

salt and pepper

## Method

❶ Preheat the grill. Chop enough parsley to fill 2 tablespoons and reserve. To make the sauce, seed and chop the chiles, then place in a food processor with the remaining parsley, onion, and garlic and process until finely chopped. Add the tomatoes and oil and process to a purée.

❷ Transfer the mixture to a pan set over very low heat, stir in the sugar, and season to taste with salt and pepper. Simmer very gently, without boiling, for 15 minutes. Transfer the sauce to an earthenware bowl and place on the side of the grill to keep warm.

❸ Rinse the shrimp under cold running water and pat dry on paper towels. Mix the reserved parsley and oil together in a dish, add the shrimp, and toss well to coat. Cook the shrimp over medium-hot coals for 3 minutes on each side, or until they have changed color. Transfer to a plate, garnish with lemon wedges, and serve with the sauce.

# Vegetables
# & Salads

# Stuffed Tomato Pockets

**An unusual filling for stuffed tomatoes, the spinach and cheese are
given extra flavor with toasted sunflower seeds.**

## serves 4

1 tbsp olive oil

2 tbsp sunflower seeds

1 onion, finely chopped

1 garlic clove, finely chopped

1 lb/450 g spinach, coarse stalks removed
and leaves shredded

pinch of freshly grated nutmeg

salt and pepper

4 beefsteak tomatoes

5 oz/140 g mozzarella cheese, diced

## Method

❶ Preheat the grill. Heat the oil in a
heavy-bottom pan. Add the sunflower
seeds and cook, stirring constantly,
for 2 minutes, or until golden. Add the
onion and cook over low heat, stirring
occasionally, for 5 minutes, or until
softened but not browned. Add the
garlic and spinach, cover, and cook for
2–3 minutes, or until the spinach has
wilted. Remove the pan from the heat
and season to taste with nutmeg, salt,
and pepper. Let cool.

❷ Using a sharp knife, cut off and reserve
a thin slice from the top of each tomato
and scoop out the flesh with a teaspoon,
taking care not to pierce the shells. Chop
the flesh and stir it into the spinach
mixture with the mozzarella cheese.

❸ Fill the tomato shells with the spinach
and cheese mixture and replace the tops.
Cut 4 squares of foil, each large enough
to enclose a tomato. Place a tomato in
the center of each square and fold up the
sides to enclose securely. Cook over hot
coals, turning occasionally, for 10 minutes.
Serve immediately in the pockets.

# Potato Fans

These garlic-flavored roast potatoes make a wonderful alternative to
baked potatoes. Allow plenty of time for cooking.

*serves 6*

6 large potatoes, scrubbed but
not peeled

2 tbsp garlic-flavored olive oil

## Method

❶ Preheat the grill. Using a sharp knife, make a series of cuts across the potatoes almost all the way through. Cut out 6 squares of foil, each large enough to enclose a potato.

❷ Place a potato on each square of foil and brush generously with the garlic-flavored oil. Fold up the sides of the foil to enclose the potatoes completely.

❸ Cook the foil pockets over hot coals, turning occasionally, for 1 hour. To serve, let cool slightly, then open the pockets and gently pinch the potatoes to open up the fans.

# Zucchini & Cheese Pockets

These delicately flavored, melt-in-the-mouth stuffed zucchini are ideal if you are serving food to both meat-eaters and vegetarians, as the pockets can be cooked in the grill embers and so avoid any contact with meat on the grill.

## serves 8

8 zucchini

1 tbsp olive oil, plus extra for brushing

4 oz/115 g feta cheese (drained weight), cut into strips

1 tablespoon finely chopped fresh mint

pepper

## Method

❶ Preheat the grill. Cut out 8 rectangles of foil, each large enough to enclose a zucchini, and brush lightly with oil. Cut a slit along the length of each zucchini and place one on each foil rectangle.

❷ Insert strips of feta cheese along the slits in the zucchini, then drizzle the oil over the top, sprinkle with the chopped mint, and season to taste with pepper. Fold in the sides of the foil and seal the edges securely to enclose the zucchini completely.

❸ Bake the zucchini pockets in the grill embers for 30 minutes. Carefully unwrap the pockets and serve immediately.

## Variation

*If you like, substitute mozzarella or fontina cheese for the feta cheese and replace the mint with the same amount of fresh parsley.*

# Vegetarian Brochettes

The great thing about tofu—apart from the fact that it is packed with protein—is its ability to absorb other flavors, in this case a mustard-and-honey-flavored glaze.

*serves 4*

2 zucchini

1 yellow bell pepper, seeded and quartered

8 oz/225 g firm tofu (drained weight)

4 cherry tomatoes

4 pearl onions

8 white mushrooms

Honey glaze

2 tbsp olive oil

1 tbsp Meaux or Dijon mustard

1 tbsp clear honey

salt and pepper

## Method

❶ Preheat the grill. Using a vegetable peeler, peel off strips of skin along the length of the zucchini to leave alternate cream and green stripes, then cut each zucchini into 8 thick slices. Cut each of the yellow bell pepper quarters in half. Cut the drained tofu into 1-inch/2.5-cm cubes.

❷ Thread the pieces of bell pepper, zucchini slices, tofu cubes, tomatoes, onions, and white mushrooms on to 4 flat metal skewers. To make the glaze, mix the oil, mustard, and honey together in a pitcher and season to taste with salt and pepper.

❸ Brush the brochettes with the honey glaze and cook over medium-hot coals, turning and brushing frequently with the glaze, for 8–10 minutes. Serve.

## Variation

*You can also make vegetable brochettes. Omit the tofu and use eggplant chunks, zucchini chunks, and small strips of red bell pepper.*

# Summer Vegetable Pockets

You can use any baby vegetables you like—pattypan squash, corn cobs, and plum tomatoes look attractive and add color. Serve with grilled meat or fish for a substantial barbecue entrée.

*serves 4*

2 lb 4 oz/1 kg mixed baby vegetables, such as carrots, pattypan squash, corn cobs, plum tomatoes, leeks, zucchini, and onions
1 lemon

½ cup unsalted butter
3 tbsp chopped mixed fresh herbs, such as parsley, thyme, and chervil
2 garlic cloves
salt and pepper

## Method

❶ Preheat the grill. Cut out 4 x 12-inch/ 30-cm squares of foil and divide the vegetables equally between them.

❷ Using a grater, finely grate the lemon rind, then squeeze the juice from the lemon and reserve until required. Place the lemon rind, butter, herbs, and garlic in a food processor and process until blended, then season to taste with salt and pepper. Alternatively, beat together in a bowl until blended.

❸ Divide the flavored butter equally between the vegetables, dotting it on top. Fold up the sides of the foil to enclose the vegetables, sealing securely. Cook over medium-hot coals, turning occasionally, for 25–30 minutes. Open the pockets, sprinkle with the reserved lemon juice, and serve immediately.

## Variation

*If baby vegetables are unavailable, then use larger vegetables cut into small pieces, such as thin sticks of zucchini and carrot, and eggplant chunks.*

# Corn on the Cob with Blue Cheese Dressing

**Corn cobs are delicious grilled over charcoal. Cook them as soon after purchase as possible because they quickly lose their sweetness as their natural sugars convert to starch.**

## *serves 6*

| | |
|---|---|
| 5 oz/140 g Danish Blue cheese | salt and pepper |
| 5 oz/140 g curd cheese | 6 corn cobs in their husks |
| ½ cup strained plain yogurt | |

## Method

❶ Preheat the grill. Crumble the Danish Blue cheese into a bowl. Beat with a wooden spoon until creamy. Beat in the curd cheese until thoroughly blended. Gradually beat in the yogurt and season to taste with salt and pepper. Cover with plastic wrap and let chill in the refrigerator until required.

❷ Fold back the husks on each corn cob and remove the silks. Smooth the husks back into place. Cut out 6 rectangles of foil, each large enough to enclose a corn cob. Wrap the corn cobs in the foil.

❸ Cook the corn cobs over hot coals, turning frequently, for 15–20 minutes. Unwrap the corn cobs and discard the foil. Peel back the husk on one side of each and trim off with a sharp knife or kitchen scissors. Serve immediately with the blue cheese dressing.

# Cajun Vegetables

These spicy vegetables would be a perfect accompaniment to some colorful Caribbean Fish Kabobs (see page 140).

*serves 4*

| | |
|---|---|
| 4 corn cobs | Spice mix |
| 2 sweet potatoes, scrubbed but not peeled | 2 tsp paprika |
| 2 tbsp butter, melted | 1 tsp ground cumin |
| | 1 tsp ground coriander |
| | 1 tsp pepper |
| | ½–1 tsp chili powder |

## Method

❶ Preheat the grill. To make the spice mix, mix all the ingredients together in a small bowl.

❷ Remove the husks and silks from the corn cobs, then cut each cob into 4 equal chunks. Cut the sweet potatoes into thick slices, but do not peel. Brush the corn chunks and sweet potato slices with melted butter and sprinkle with some spice mix.

❸ Cook the corn cobs and sweet potatoes over medium-hot coals, turning frequently, for 12–15 minutes. Brush with more melted butter and sprinkle with extra spice mixture during cooking. Transfer the corn and sweet potatoes to a large serving plate and serve immediately.

# Prune, Apricot & Onion Skewers

These flavorsome, fruity skewers go well with plain grilled pork chops, duck breasts, lamb steaks, or kabobs, as their sweetness counteracts the richness of the meat.

## *serves 4*

1 lb/450 g pearl onions

6 oz/175 g no-soak prunes, pitted

8 oz/225 g dried apricots, pitted

2-inch/5-cm cinnamon stick

1 cup white wine

2 tbsp chili sauce

2 tbsp corn oil

## Method

❶ Cut the tops off the onions and peel off the skin. Reserve until required. Place the prunes, apricots, cinnamon stick, and wine in a heavy-bottom pan and bring to a boil. Reduce the heat and simmer for 5 minutes. Drain, reserving the cooking liquid and cinnamon stick, and set aside the fruits until cool enough to handle.

❷ Return the cooking liquid and cinnamon stick to the pan, return to a boil, and boil until reduced by half. Remove the pan from the heat and remove and discard the cinnamon stick. Stir in the chili sauce and oil.

❸ Thread the prunes, apricots, and onions on to several flat metal skewers. Cook over medium-hot coals, turning and brushing frequently with the wine mixture, for 10 minutes. Serve immediately.

# Eggplant with Tzatziki

This makes a delicious appetizer for a barbecue party or can be served as part of a vegetarian barbecue meze with Stuffed Tomato Pockets (see page 158), or Zucchini & Cheese Pockets (see page 162).

*serves 4*

2 tbsp olive oil

salt and pepper

2 eggplants, thinly sliced

Tzatziki

½ cucumber

1 garlic clove

4 scallions

1¼ cups strained plain yogurt

3 tbsp chopped fresh mint

salt and pepper

fresh mint sprigs, to garnish

## Method

❶ Preheat the grill. To make the Tzatziki, follow Steps 1 and 2 on page 16. Transfer the Tzatziki to a serving bowl, cover with plastic wrap, and let chill in the refrigerator until required.

❷ Season the oil with salt and pepper, then brush the eggplant slices with the oil.

❸ Cook the eggplant over hot coals for 5 minutes on each side, brushing with more oil, if necessary. Transfer to a large serving plate and serve immediately with the Tzatziki, garnished with a mint sprig.

# Tropical Rice Salad

Rice salads are always popular and this colorful, fruity mixture goes especially well
with barbecued meat or chicken.

*serves 4*

generous ½ cup long-grain rice

salt

4 scallions

8 oz/225 g canned pineapple pieces in
natural juice

1 cup canned corn kernels, drained

2 red bell peppers, seeded and diced

3 tbsp golden raisins

Dressing

1 tbsp peanut oil

1 tbsp hazelnut oil

1 tbsp light soy sauce

1 garlic clove, finely chopped

1 tsp chopped fresh gingerroot

salt and pepper

## Method

❶ Cook the rice in a large pan of lightly
salted boiling water for 15 minutes, or
until tender. Drain thoroughly and rinse
under cold running water. Place the rice
in a large serving bowl.

❷ Using a sharp knife, finely slice the
scallions. Drain the pineapple pieces,
reserving the juice in a pitcher. Add the
pineapple pieces, corn, peppers, scallions,
and golden raisins to the rice and mix
together lightly.

❸ Add all the dressing ingredients to the
reserved pineapple juice, whisking well,
and season to taste with salt and pepper.
Pour the dressing over the salad and toss
until the salad is thoroughly coated.
Serve immediately.

## Variation

*Try other flavored nut oils, such as walnut oil or
sesame oil. You can also substitute sunflower-seed
oil for the peanut oil, if you prefer.*

# Tabbouleh

This Middle Eastern salad is increasingly fashionable. It is a classic accompaniment to lamb, but goes well with most grilled meat.

*serves 4*

¾ cup bulgur wheat

3 tbsp extra virgin olive oil

4 tbsp lemon juice

salt and pepper

4 scallions

1 green bell pepper, seeded and sliced

4 tomatoes, chopped

2 tbsp chopped fresh parsley

2 tbsp chopped fresh mint

8 black olives, pitted

fresh mint sprigs, to garnish

## Method

❶ Place the bulgur wheat in a large bowl and add enough cold water to cover. Let stand for 30 minutes, or until the wheat has doubled in size. Drain well and press out as much liquid as possible. Spread the wheat out on paper towels to dry.

❷ Place the wheat in a serving bowl. Mix the oil and lemon juice together in a pitcher and season to taste with salt and pepper. Pour the lemon mixture over the wheat and let marinate for 1 hour.

❸ Using a sharp knife, finely slice the scallions, then add to the salad with the bell pepper, tomatoes, parsley, and mint and toss lightly to mix. Top the salad with the olives, garnish with mint sprigs, and serve immediately.

## Variation

*Use different types of fresh tomatoes—try vine-ripened tomatoes, which have a delicate, sweet flavor, or cherry tomatoes, cut in half.*

# Cheese & Walnut Pasta Salad

This is an ideal salad to serve with a barbecue, as it is not just a pasta salad, which can seem a little mundane, but also includes a colorful mix of crisp salad greens.

### serves 4

3½ cups dried fusilli

salt and pepper

8 oz/225 g Gorgonzola cheese

3½ oz/100 g mixed salad greens, such as oakleaf lettuce, radicchio, baby spinach, arugula, and mâche

1 cup walnut halves

4 tbsp sunflower-seed or corn oil

2 tbsp walnut oil

2 tbsp red wine vinegar

## Method

❶ Cook the pasta in a large pan of lightly salted boiling water for 8–10 minutes, or until tender, but still firm to the bite. Drain, rinse under cold running water, and drain again.

❷ Using a sharp knife, cut the cheese into cubes. Place the salad greens in a large serving bowl and add the cooked pasta. Sprinkle the cheese on top.

❸ Preheat the broiler to medium. Place the walnut halves on a large cookie sheet and cook under the broiler for a few minutes, or until lightly toasted. Let cool. Mix the sunflower-seed oil, walnut oil, and vinegar together in a pitcher and season to taste with salt and pepper. Pour the dressing over the salad, toss lightly to coat, then top with the toasted walnuts.

# Red & Green Salad

**Beet and orange is a classic combination and here they are mixed with tender baby spinach leaves to make a dramatic and colorful warm salad.**

## *serves 4*

1 lb 7 oz/650 g cooked beets, peeled

3 tbsp extra virgin olive oil

juice of 1 orange

1 tsp superfine sugar

1 tsp fennel seeds

salt and pepper

4 oz/115 g baby spinach leaves

## Method

❶ Using a sharp knife, dice the cooked beet and reserve until required. Heat the oil in a small, heavy-bottom pan. Add the orange juice, sugar, and fennel seeds and season to taste with salt and pepper. Stir constantly until the sugar has dissolved.

❷ Add the reserved beets to the pan and stir gently to coat. Remove the pan from the heat.

❸ Arrange the baby spinach leaves and warmed beets on a plate and serve immediately.

Desserts

# Mixed Fruit Kabobs

You can use almost any firm-fleshed fruit to make these colorful, quick and easy kabobs. Remember to soak the wooden skewers in cold water before using to prevent burning.

### *serves 4*

2 nectarines, halved and pitted

2 kiwifruit

4 red plums

1 mango, peeled, halved, and pitted

2 bananas, peeled and thickly sliced

8 strawberries, hulled

1 tbsp clear honey

3 tbsp Cointreau

## Method

❶ Cut the nectarine halves in half again and place in a large, shallow dish. Peel and quarter the kiwifruit. Cut the plums in half and remove the pits. Cut the mango flesh into chunks and add to the dish with the kiwifruit, plums, bananas, and strawberries.

❷ Mix the honey and Cointreau together in a pitcher until well blended. Pour the mixture over the fruit and toss lightly to coat. Cover with plastic wrap and let marinate in the refrigerator for 1 hour.

❸ Preheat the grill. Drain the fruit, reserving the marinade. Thread the fruit on to several presoaked wooden skewers and cook over medium-hot coals, turning and brushing frequently with the reserved marinade, for 5–7 minutes, then serve.

# Barbecued Baked Apples

**When they are wrapped in foil, apples bake to perfection on the grill and make a delightful finale to any meal.**

## serves 4

4 medium cooking apples

2 x 1-inch/2.5-cm pieces preserved ginger, chopped

¼ cup walnuts, chopped

⅓ cup ground almonds

¼ cup raw brown sugar

5-6 cherries, chopped

1 tbsp Amaretto (optional)

4 tbsp butter

whipped cream or plain yogurt, to serve

## Method

❶ Preheat the grill. Core the apples and, using a sharp knife, score each one around the middle to prevent the apple skins splitting while cooking.

❷ To make the filling, mix the ginger, nuts, sugar, cherries, and Amaretto, if using, together in a small bowl.

❸ Spoon some filling mixture into each apple, pushing it down into the hollowed-out core. Mound a little of the filling mixture on top of each apple.

❹ Place each apple on a large square of double-thickness foil and generously dot all over with the butter. Gather up and seal the foil so that the filled apple is completely enclosed.

❺ Grill the foil pockets containing the apples over hot coals for 25-30 minutes, or until tender.

❻ Transfer the apples to warmed individual serving plates. Serve with lashings of whipped cream or plain yogurt.

## Variation

*If the coals are dying down, place the foil pockets directly on to the coals, raking them up around the apples.*

# Banana Sizzles

**Bananas are particularly sweet and delicious when grilled—
and conveniently come with their own protective wrapping.**

### *serves 4*

3 tbsp butter, softened

2 tbsp dark rum

1 tbsp orange juice

4 tbsp raw brown sugar

pinch of ground cinnamon

4 bananas

orange zest, to decorate

## Method

❶ Preheat the grill. Beat the butter with the rum, orange juice, sugar, and cinnamon in a small bowl until thoroughly blended and smooth.

❷ Place the bananas, without peeling, over hot coals and cook, turning frequently, for 6–8 minutes, or until the skins are blackened.

❸ Transfer the bananas to serving plates, slit the skins, and cut partially through the flesh lengthwise. Divide the flavored butter between the bananas, decorate with orange zest, and serve.

# Recipe List

- Aïoli *14* • Anchovy, Olive & Cheese Triangles *62* • Baba Ghanoush *26*
- Bacon Koftas *122* • Bacon-Wrapped Trout *148* • Banana Sizzles *190*
- Barbecued Baked Apples *188* • Best Ever Burgers *108* • Böreks *54*
- Bruschetta *94* • Cajun Vegetables *170* • Caribbean Crab Cakes *60*
- Caribbean Fish Kabobs *140* • Chargrilled Devils *152* • Cheese & Apricot Morsels *58*
- Cheese & Bean Pâté *34* • Cheese & Walnut Pasta Salad *180* • Cheese Straws *48*
- Chicken Tikka *126* • Corn-on-the-Cob with Blue Cheese Dressing *168*
- Deep-Fried Shrimp Balls *64* • Devils & Angels on Horseback *82*
- Easy Nibbles *46* • Egg & Tapenade Toasties *42* • Eggplant with Tzatziki *174*
- Fabulous Frankfurter Skewers *124* • Filled Croustades *44* • Fruity Duck *136*
- Guacamole *20* • Honey & Mustard Drumsticks *74* • Hot Red Chicken *130*
- Hummus with Lebanese Seed Bread *24* • Indonesian Peanut Fritters *88*
- Little Feta & Spinach Crescents *56* • Luxury Cheeseburgers *110*
- Meatballs on Sticks *120* • Mini Artichoke Pizzas *92* • Mini Pepperoni Pizzas *90*
- Minted Lamb Steaks *114* • Mixed Fruit Kabobs *186*
- Moroccan Pickled Vegetables *52* • Mushroom & Chestnut Pâté *32*
- Normandy Brochettes *116* • Orange & Lemon Peppered Angler Fish *146*
- Pigs in Blankets *96* • Potato Fans *160* • Prune, Apricot & Onion Skewers *172*
- Quiche Lorraine *50* • Quick Chicken Liver Pâté with Melba Toast *28*
- Rack & Ruin *112* • Red & Green Salad *182* • Red Bell Pepper Dip *22*
- Sage & Lemon Squab Chickens *128* • Salmon with Mango Salsa *142*
- San Francisco Wings *84* • Sausage Rolls *72* • Sausages with Barbecue Sauce *118*
- Seafood Phyllo Pockets *80* • Sicilian Shrimp *66* • Sizzling Scallops *150*
- Smoked Fish Pâté *30* • Spanish Shrimp *154* • Spareribs *86*
- Spicy Seafood Kabobs *78* • Stuffed Grape Leaves *68* • Stuffed Sardines *144*
- Stuffed Tomato Pockets *158* • Summer Vegetable Pockets *166*
- Tabasco Steaks with Parsley Butter *106* • Tabbouleh *178* • Taramasalata *18*
- Tarragon Turkey *134* • Three-Flavor Pinwheels *40*
- Traditional English Potted Shrimp *36* • Tropical Rice Salad *176* • Turkey Rolls *132*
- Tzatziki *16* • Vegetable Samosas *70* • Vegetarian Brochettes *164*
- Zucchini & Cheese Pockets *162*